MAKING EUROPE
UNCONQUERABLE

A book from the
Program on Nonviolent Sanctions
in Conflict and Defense
Center for International Affairs
Harvard University
Cambridge, Massachusetts
and the
Albert Einstein Institution
Cambridge, Massachusetts

MAKING EUROPE UNCONQUERABLE
The Potential of Civilian-based Deterrence and Defense

GENE SHARP

Program on Nonviolent Sanctions
in Conflict and Defense
Center for International Affairs
Harvard University

and the

Albert Einstein Institution

With a Foreword by
George F. Kennan

BALLINGER PUBLISHING COMPANY
Cambridge, Massachusetts
A Subsidiary of Harper & Row Publishing, Inc.

UK   Taylor & Francis Ltd, 4 John St., London WCIN 2ET

USA   Ballinger Publishing Company, 54 Church Street, Harvard Square,
Cambridge, MA 02138

British Library Cataloguing in Publication Data

Sharp, Gene.
Making Europe unconquerable: the potential of civilian-based
deterrence and defence.
1. Military occupation.   2. Passive resistance—Europe. I. Title.
303.6'1   U163
ISBN 0-85066-329-6 (softback)
ISBN 0-85066-336-9 (hardback)

Library of Congress Cataloging in Publication Data

Sharp, Gene.
Making Europe unconquerable.
Bibliography: p.
Includes index.
1. Europe—Defenses. 2. Passive resistance. I. Title.
II. Title: Civilian-based deterrence and defense.
UA646.S47 1985   355'.03304   85-12592
ISBN 0-85066-329-6 (softback)
ISBN 0-85066-336-9 (hardback)

Printed in the United States of America

*"Paralysis, rather than destruction,
is the true aim in war*, and the more
far reaching in its effects."
— Sir Basil Liddell Hart*

---

*Sir Basil Liddell Hart, *When Britain Goes to War* (London: Faber and Faber, 1935),
p. 106.

CONTENTS

FOREWORD

Professor Gene Sharp has given several years of study to the possibilities of deterrence and resistance by civilians as a conceivable alternative, or partial alternative, to the traditional, purely military concepts of national defense that have so long prevailed and continue to prevail in European countries. He has restricted the range of applicability of his researches and reflections to Europe, and has directed them, within those limits, primarily to the neutral countries such as Austria and Finland. But his study is intended to apply, at least hypothetically, to such other countries, now members of one or the other of the great nuclear alliances, as might in some distant future succeed in detaching themselves from the alliance in question and thus find themselves compelled to devise an independent defense policy that makes sense with regard to the military and political realities of the present day. The question addressed in this book is essentially this: Where is the peace-loving, nonaggressive, and nonaligned country to find the maximum security against outside interference and domination in a world where war itself, and therefore the traditional preparations for war, have lost so much of their rationale as instruments of national policy?

The answer in the NATO establishment (and perhaps also, although with diminished conviction and enthusiasm, in the Soviet one, too) would be: in the nuclear deterrent, of course. Either, one would say, you have your own nuclear arsenal, or you ally yourself with someone else who has one.

Mr. Sharp challenges (quite correctly in my opinion) the validity of this supposed alternative. Not only is the nuclear deterrent by its very nature dangerously unstable but it is not really a means of defense. In the concept of nuclear deterrence, Mr. Sharp notes, "the capacity to defend in order to deter has been replaced by the capability to destroy massively without the ability to defend." Beyond this there is, for any country wishing to go the nuclear road, the necessity of choosing between the development of a nuclear arsenal of one's own, at vast expense and in defiance of the international effort to restrict proliferation, and the acceptance of an alliance with some existing nuclear power—a relationship bound, as experience has shown, to raise the unanswerable question about whose interests, those of the protector or those of the nominally protected, are eventually to prevail in a moment of crisis so brief as to be responsive only to the impulses of the computer.

Finally, as Mr. Sharp also points out, to create a nuclear arsenal or to accept someone else's missiles on one's own territory is to increase immensely, from a point of near zero to a very high level, the danger that in any sort of a nuclear conflict one's own country will become a likely target. Mr. Sharp could even have strengthened his case, in this respect, by pointing out that the Soviet leaders have repeatedly and specifically affirmed that they would never use nuclear weapons against any country that did not itself deploy them or permit them to be deployed on its own territory—an assurance that deserves greater credence than it has generally received, not only because there would be no reason to put out such a statement exclusively to deceive, but also because, given the general irrationality of the nuclear weapon, that policy in question makes perfectly good sense.

Thus for a nonnuclear country determined to pursue an independent policy but required to live under the shadow of the nuclear competition of the two superpowers, the nuclear option is not a hopeful one. But neither, for that matter, is an exclusive reliance on the traditional concepts of defense with "conventional" weapons. In an age of long-range striking power by aircraft, by missiles, even by long-range artillery, the idea of defense at the frontier has lost its reality. Beyond that, such is now the destructive power of even non-nuclear weapons that a war fought with them, particularly a defensive war presumably conducted largely on one's own territory, promises nothing but a degree of devastation that makes a mockery of the very idea of military victory. Here we simply get back to the fact that war, generally, as among the industrially advanced and technologically sophisticated countries, can no longer serve any useful purpose—not even that of a defense.

It did not, actually, take the post-World War II advances in weapons technology to establish this fact. It is inescapably clear that in the two great European wars of this century there were, in reality, no victors. These were, in effect, simply senseless orgies of destruction. The damages they inflicted, on the nominal victor and the defeated alike, were far greater and more insidious than people were even aware of at the time, reaching as they did into the spiritual and genetic as well as the purely military and physical realms. It is idle for the independent European country of this day to suppose that by entering into a new and even more horrible round of such carnage it could protect anything worth protecting.

These two supposed alternatives for an independent defense on the part of the unaligned Continental country are therefore, when looked at carefully, no alternatives at all. It is not surprising, in these circumstances, that people's minds should turn to the question whether there might not be some means of defense that would at least hold out hope of avoiding the sheer physical disasters that both of these supposed alternatives invite. It is this necessity that has led to Professor Sharp's inquiry into the possibilities and limitations of civilian-based defense; and it would be unfair to judge it in any way other than in relation to the unpromising nature of these two, and only, visible alternatives. It is worth bearing in mind, as one reads his book, that however one assesses the possibilities of civilian-based defense, the nature of the available alternatives is such that it would not take much to be preferable to them.

Mr. Sharp's study addresses itself, as its subtitle (*The Potential of Civilian-based Deterrence and Defense*) implies, both to deterrence and to resistance if deterrence fails. The two are of course closely connected; but each requires separate treatment, and receives it.

Deterrence, in this instance, is of particular importance. For the study starts, as so much conventional military thinking fails to do, from the assumption that the presumptive attacker is motivated not just by a blind urge to destroy for destruction's sake but rather by a wholly rational desire to gain domination over the political life of the victim country and to use that domination to his own advantage. And here, of course, is where the reactions of the civilian population—its will to resist and the preparation it has been given for doing so—come in. To deny this is to fly in the face of the historical evidence. For if we consider the failure of other powers to attack Switzerland during the two world wars, the failure of the Soviet Union to occupy Finland in the wake of their conflicts during World War II, and the similar abstention by Moscow from attacking Yugoslavia after that country's break with the Soviet Union in 1948, we can see that calculations relating to the respective country's presumptive powers of internal resistance, while certainly not the only considerations that played a part, occupied a prominent place among those that determined the final decision.

The successful imposition of foreign domination over a given country requires the ability of the dominating power to find, from among the population of that country, a faction either so inspired ideologically or so successfully cowed as to serve as a puppet government. It then requires that this faction should have the capacity to recruit the requisite indigenous bureaucracy, and to compel the population to accept and respect its authority. But whether these conditions can or cannot be met is something that will be importantly affected by the extent and effectiveness of the training, indoctrination, and general preparation for resistance that the population has received in advance of the event. This, in turn, is something the potential aggressor is likely to have a fair idea of before he takes the decision whether or not to attack; and his decision is bound to be affected by his assessment of its importance.

As for resistance itself if deterrence fails, there are a great many possible forms of this (Mr. Sharp has himself identified nearly two hundred of them). Some of these may be overt and largely spontaneous; others require the most highly centralized leadership, training, and direction. Some are designed to have military effect; others are directed solely to civilian administration. Some require mass participation; others can be conducted only conspiratorially, by carefully selected and highly trained individuals. The mix to be chosen in any given instance must depend on the nature of the country in question and the peculiarities of the prevailing situation. To select among these, and to conduct careful advance planning and preparation for their implementation, is a function that lies at the heart of civilian-based defense as Mr. Sharp sees it; and it is precisely in this respect that his reflections are most importantly innovative.

For seldom, if ever, in the contests of the past, has there been any such thing as this careful advance preparation. The resistance movements that made themselves felt during the Second World War were almost without exception ones that had to be improvised under conditions of extreme danger and difficulty—under the eyes and guns, that is, of the occupier. There can be no doubt that had they had the sort of advance preparation this study envisages, their effectiveness would have been increased several times over. Lines of command would have been known; effective channels of communication would have existed; there would have been adequate caches of weapons and supplies; ordinary citizens would have had guidance and instruction as to how to behave; given types of action would have been rehearsed and prepared.

Skeptics may point to the long endurance of the Soviet hegemony in Eastern Europe as evidence of the hopelessness of civilian resistance to domination by a strong outside power. But again, what they will be citing as an example is not at all what Mr. Sharp has in mind. There was, in those instances, no possibility whatsoever for advance preparation—quite the contrary. What the Soviet authorities found before them, as their armies overran this great region, was a territory where all semblance of real indigenous authority had already been swept away by the preceding Nazi-German occupation. It is often forgotten that it was not the Russians but the Nazis who destroyed the prewar status quo in that part of the world, and with it all social and political stability. What the Russians found there was in fact a territory ideally prepared to receive just the sort of domination they were desirous of establishing—a situation, in short, just the opposite of the one Mr. Sharp has in mind when he examines the possibilities of a resistance well prepared in advance by an indigenous government enjoying the confidence of the people. For this concept, there are, in fact, few examples. It is a modern concept, addressed to the unprecedented conditions of this modern age.

I am not in total agreement with all of Mr. Sharp's argument. There are places where the emphasis, in my view, could have been usefully shifted. I would have placed more weight on highly centralized, clandestine direction, less on spontaneous mass action. I am not sure that the nature of civilian defense planning should be so widely publicized as the author of the book would seem to envisage. I am less sanguine than he is about the possibilities for demoralizing the armed forces of an intruder. But these are minor differences, particularly if we take into account the limitations Mr. Sharp has placed on his own conclusions.

There is, of course, in this endangered world, no such thing as absolute defense for anyone; and Mr. Sharp advances no claim that a civilian-based system would provide this. He does not even claim that civilian-based defense could usefully constitute the *only* component of an adequate defense policy. He recognizes that it might have to be combined, at one stage or another, with the actions of certain types of regular military forces. He does not even depict his own conclusions as definitive. His plea is only that civilian-based defense has a legitimate place among the options open to the sort of country he is talking about; that this place is plainly larger than has been generally supposed; and that its possibilities ought to be more carefully studied and considered than they have been in the past. His primary purpose in writing the book was, he says, "to make civilian-based deterrence and defense a thinkable policy which is recognized as meriting further research, policy studies, and an evaluation." And for this, he makes a reasonably good case.

But he must not expect, just for this reason, that the effort to win understanding for his views will be easy going. It goes against the grain of all established strategic thinking. The professional military establishments will brush it off with incredulity, if not with contempt. It will arouse in many circles the same skepticism, and perhaps the same derision, that this reviewer brought down upon himself when he had the temerity to advance somewhat similar ideas in a widely publicized radio lecture delivered over the facilities of the BBC many years ago.

But the view advanced in this book deserves consideration, if only because of the bankruptcy of all the visible alternatives to it. It might just be that in a world where the devices of long-range military destruction have proliferated beyond all reason, the greatest security any country can hope to have, imperfect as it is, will be found to lie primarily in its confidence in itself, in its readiness to leave other people alone and to go its own way, in its willingness to accept the sort of social discipline that a civilian-based defense implies—in a stance, in other words, that offers minimal incentive to foreign military intrusion but promises to make things difficult, painful, and unprofitable for any power that decides, nevertheless, to intrude. Such principles may not be everywhere applicable. Nowhere may they be the complete answer to the problems at hand. But beggars, in this world of destructive power unlimited, cannot always be choosers. And Mr. Sharp's approach, certainly more humane and in a small way more hopeful than many others, deserves at least to be given a hearing.

To see things in this way will require, however, a rather basic change in the view hundreds of millions of people have been taught to take of the sources of national security and of the means by which it may be usefully promoted. The new view would be one that looks primarily inward—to the quality of the respective society, to the character of its institutions, to its social discipline and civic morale, rather than outward to the effectiveness of its armed forces—for the true sources of its strength and its security. It suggests, in Mr. Sharp's words, "the direct defense of society as such—its principles, free institutions, and liberties—rather than a futile attempt to defend territory as an indirect means to defend the society." It raises, in fact, the question whether any society can be stronger in relation to others than it is to itself.

What is implied here is no less than a change in political philosophy. For it taps, as Mr. Sharp says in his final passages, "a crucial insight into the nature of power"—namely, that

> all political power is rooted in and continually dependent upon the cooperation and obedience of the subjects and institutions of the society. . . . It is indeed possible for whole societies to apply that insight . . . against internal and foreign aggressors, and to triumph. . . . With effort, risks, and costs, it is possible for Europeans—and all peoples—to make themselves politically indigestible to would-be tyrants. The process has already begun.

Perhaps those words overstate the case; but if so, not greatly. One ends the reading of the book wondering whether, if this change in political philosophy were to take place, it might not have wider effects than just those that relate to the concepts of national security—whether many other things might not also change, and, in the main, usefully so.

George F. Kennan

PREFACE

'Making Europe Unconquerable' offers a fresh approach to Western European security problems. It sketches the main characteristics of the policy of civilian-based defense, and outlines its relevance for Western European countries.

This book maintains that this unconventional policy merits full public consideration, scholarly research, and strategic examination to determine whether, as is claimed, it could deter and dissuade attacks by the Soviet Union or from other foreign or internal sources and defend successfully against them if they nevertheless occurred.

If it could, then European security problems would be drastically altered, American involvement (including military and financial) would become largely unnecessary, and the dangers of nuclear war in Europe would be lifted. An alternative defense policy is required both to provide effective deterrence and defense to deal with existing and future security threats and also to make it possible for Europeans to give up dependence on military weaponry which itself threatens their survival. It is almost certainly impossible to divest ourselves of present military systems unless we possess alternative means to deter and defeat aggression.

For supporters of present national and NATO policies in Western Europe, that means a capability to deter and defend successfully against a possible attack from the Soviet Union.

This book is largely an attempt to point toward an answer to the question whether deterrence and defense can be provided by a different type of weapons system, which uses neither conventional military weapons nor nuclear ones.

Western European security problems and how they ought to be solved are topics which ought to be approached by Americans with greater caution than is commonly the case, especially among those American officials and strategists who favor a policy which prepares for using nuclear weapons in Europe to "defend" Europeans from Soviet aggression.

I am an American and this is a book about European security policy. I ask, however, that readers in European countries evaluate the book according to its merits, not my citizenship. This plea is not made simply on the basis of intellectual freedom or the idea that sometimes an outsider may have fresher insights than persons immersed in their immediate situation. My long study of the nature of nonviolent struggle and its potential for defense, my ten years of living in England and Norway, my doctoral studies at Oxford, and my visits to most other Western European countries may together provide a background, sensitivity, and perspective not available to everyone. The content of the book should be evaluated on the basis of how satisfactorily it addresses the security problems of Western European countries in face of the reality of modern war. This small volume cannot provide a blueprint for the application of this policy for each individual European country, much less for Western Europe as a whole. (The title of the book is not 'Europe Made Unconquerable.') The development of detailed scenarios and plans for the many possible contingencies requires the participation of analysts, strategists, social scientists, and citizens of diverse occupations and professions in each country which might adopt this policy in whole or in part. The participation is also required of those persons who would examine the policy for possible application by several Western European countries simultaneously or by NATO as a whole.

This book is designed to stimulate and assist that future examination and development, not to pre-empt it.

'Making Europe Unconquerable' is intended to make civilian-based deterrence and defense a thinkable policy which is recognized as meriting further research, policy studies, and evaluation. Civilian-based defense is a policy still in the process of development. In most (if not all) countries, serious consideration of this policy is more likely to be advanced by research, policy studies, and strategic analyses of its potential than by a "campaign" being launched advocating its immediate adoption. There is no substitute for the hard, slow work of expanding our knowledge and understanding of the relevant phenomena and seeking answers to the many difficult problems which arise in applying this policy.

While that work proceeds, it is also very important for people in all walks of life and in all societies to learn more about this policy. We all need to think about its possible role in dissuading attacks of diverse kinds and providing defense when needed. Can this policy provide effective defense against aggressive dictatorships while avoiding the dangers of nuclear annihilation? Much depends on how many people seriously seek an answer to that question.

ACKNOWLEDGMENTS

This work was not originally planned as a book. I initially simply sought publication as a pamphlet of a chapter commissioned by the United Nations Educational, Scientific, and Cultural Organization but which is now not to be published by that body. That was an introduction to the policy of civilian-based defense, deliberately void of political context. Friends at the Institute for World Order (now the World Policy Institute) accepted it but asked that for their edition political context be restored, and I agreed to add some material on Western Europe. That was three years ago, and the pamphlet has long since become a book. In the meantime the topic and the unpublished book have aroused interest both in Europe and America. A fuller appreciation of how civilian-based defense can defeat powerful military aggressors can be gained from study of how nonviolent struggle more generally works against repressive systems. For this, readers are referred especially to my 'The Politics of Nonviolent Action' and 'Social Power and Political Freedom,' and to the related book 'Gandhi as a Political Strategist.'

Many of the ideas and discussions of the characteristics of civilian-based defense in this book will be developed more fully in my 'Post-Military Defense,' to be published by Princeton University Press.

For both substantive and editorial suggestions, I am grateful to my assistant Robert Irwin, Sherle Schwenninger of the World Policy Institute, Charles H. Hamilton, and William B. Vogele. I am also grateful for editorial suggestions to Philip Bogdonoff, Gregory Bates, and Carl Etnier (also assistants), Stephen Maikowski of the World Policy Institute, and Dr. John Cheney of Taylor & Francis. Robert Irwin and Barbara Doughty helped edit the whole manuscript in its final drafts. None of these, however, is responsible for my errors of judgment! Schuyler Engel provided important help, and Jennifer Bing, Gregory Bates, and Philip Bogdonoff solved various problems with ingenuity and persistence. Steve Csipke ably prepared the index. Dr. Susan Abrams played a vital role in the promotion of the first edition and has ably assisted in the production of this new edition.

I am also grateful to those individuals and small foundations — which prefer to remain nameless — that by their financial support have enabled my work to continue over the years, even though they have often hoped that more affluent sources would take over the task!

Harvard University's Center for International Affairs has for most of the years since 1965 provided an academic home for my research and writing, and Southeastern Massachusetts University was my teaching university from 1970 to 1986. The administrators and faculty of both institutions have provided encouragement and various types of assistance for which I am grateful.

The establishment within Harvard's Center for International Affairs of the Program on Nonviolent Sanctions in Conflict and Defense in May 1983 has made possible the expansion of my work on nonviolent alternatives and the completion of this book. In addition, the recently founded Albert Einstein Institution, which is now my primary affiliation, provided support toward the completion of this work.

It is gratifying that the initial response to the book in the United States has led Ballinger Publishing Company to prepare this new American edition only a few months after the initial release.

I am very grateful to Professor Kennan and *The New York Review of Books* for their permission to reprint his review as a Foreword to this edition.

The work will have been worthwhile if the book provokes widespread reexamination of what is required to prevent and defeat attacks on Western European societies in an age of modern dictatorships and weapons of mass destruction.

1 MEETING EUROPE'S DEFENSE NEEDS

THE NEED FOR DEFENSE CAPACITY

The history of this century demonstrates that the countries of Europe need effective means to prevent and defend against foreign and domestic attacks and to preserve their independence, their chosen political systems, ways of life, and liberties. Both the governments and populations of the countries of Western Europe have consequently sought to ensure their security by self-reliant efforts and by joint action in alliances.

Over the decades many lives, much intelligence, great energy, and vast resources have been expended to ensure for Europeans of various countries security against attacks and to provide them with effective defense in crises. Yet today, both supporters and critics of present security policies for Western European countries have good reason to be dissatisfied. It can be convincingly argued, on the one hand, that present policies are inadequate to ensure their objectives against the military might of the Soviet Union. In some countries, possible internal threats such as coups d'état or executive usurpations are not even addressed. On the other hand, it is at least equally clear that present military policies to deal with external threats leave many Europeans with deep fears that if and when these policies are applied against an actual attack, Europe will be devastated and many

1

millions will die in a nuclear "exchange" having nothing to do with defense. Today's military security policies leave many people with grounds for deep insecurities.

The dual dangers of ineffective deterrence and defense and of annihilation of the populations being defended ought to make us search vigorously for a superior policy which could increase our security while drastically reducing potential casualties. With rare exceptions, that search has not been launched, and it is even widely assumed that such a policy could not be found. Indeed, it is arguable that within the framework of military assumptions, no such policy exists. Thus far, few people have been able to think outside the framework of military assumptions.

A very different policy which uses nonmilitary means to deter and defend against attack is being developed, however. It is claimed that this policy can both reduce the likelihood of attacks and increase actual defense capacity, while not inviting a nuclear or conventional holocaust.

This book is mostly about that policy, called "civilian-based defense," and its relevance for meeting the security needs of the countries of Western Europe. In this policy, the whole population and the society's institutions become the fighting forces. Their weaponry consists of a vast variety of forms of psychological, economic, social, and political resistance and counter-attack. This policy aims to deter attacks and to defend against them by preparations to make the society unrulable by would-be tyrants and aggressors. The trained population and the society's institutions would be prepared to deny the attackers their objectives and to make consolidation of political control impossible. These aims would be achieved by applying massive and selective noncooperation and defiance. In addition, where possible, the defending country would aim to create maximum international problems for the attackers and to subvert the reliability of their troops and functionaries.

This policy is clearly unorthodox by contemporary military standards. However, military solutions to defense problems remain contemporary political orthodoxy only because people concerned with security questions ignore, dismiss, or belittle the long European experience of improvised civilian resistance using such methods against foreign aggression and domination and against internal takeovers.

Civilian-based defense is rooted in such experience, both in Europe and elsewhere. The full record of these other national defense struggles has not been compiled, and often relatively little attention has been given by historians to these nonmilitary campaigns.

Let us just mention some of the major cases of such resistance from the nineteenth and twentieth centuries. Following defeat of a military uprising under Kossuth, Hungarians shifted to nonviolent means and resisted Austrian rule from 1850 to 1867. They built indigenous economic, social and political institutions and applied many forms of political noncooperation, including refusal to pay taxes and to bid at auctions on seized property. From 1898 to 1905 Finns, ruled by the Tsarist Empire, resisted Russification and military conscription in efforts to retain and assert their national integrity.

In 1920, during the early months of the new democratic Weimar Republic, Germans used popular defiance, the general strike, and massive political noncooperation to defend their new liberal democracy from the anti-democratic Kapp 'Putsch.' In 1923, only a few years after the battles of the First World War, the Germans struggled against the Franco-Belgian occupation of the Ruhr with a deliberate government-initiated nonviolent strategy of economic and political noncooperation.

During the Second World War—in such occupied countries as the Netherlands, Norway and Denmark—patriots resisted their Nazi overlords and internal puppets by such weapons as underground newspapers, labor slowdowns, general strikes, refusal of collaboration, social boycotts of German troops and quislings, and noncooperation with fascist controls and efforts to restructure their societies' institutions. Many of the efforts to save Jews from the Holocaust in several countries (Belgium, the Netherlands, Norway, Denmark, France, Italy, Bulgaria) and even in Berlin took nonviolent forms, such as refusing to register or report for deportation, offering refuge, organizing escape routes, strikes, and public demonstrations.

In 1961 the French government of Charles de Gaulle was threatened by the Algiers generals' coup. Public demonstrations against the prospect of overthrow of the government in Paris, major symbolic strikes, and massive noncooperation by French soldiers against their mutinous officers dissolved the usurpation without civil war.

When the Soviet Union led a Warsaw Pact invasion of Czechoslovakia to halt efforts to create "socialism with a human face" and to restore a hard-line Communist Party rule, despite lack of preparations the society waged a massive campaign of nonviolent resistance to the invasion and occupation. This included subversion of Soviet troops, symbolic strikes, public defiance by Party and government institutions, resistance newspapers and radio broadcasts, refusal of collaboration, and street demonstrations. The resistance lasted eight months.

A search of the history of these and other European countries is likely to reveal additional neglected national defense struggles. In light of the gravity of both the security threats to Western Europe and the limitations and destructive capacity of military options, such cases merit careful consideration as possible prototypes of an alternative defense policy.

Some of the above cases resulted in defeats, some in successes, some in mixed results. All were improvised. These civilian defenders lacked the advantages of advance preparations and trained fighting forces which are seen as essential for military combat. Exponents of civilian-based defense maintain that the effectiveness of improvised resistance can be significantly increased by preparing and training the population, informed by basic research, problem-solving research, and policy and feasibility studies.

This research has already begun on a small scale in a few Western European countries and the United States. Political and governmental interest has often exceeded the progress in research. In Sweden, Switzerland, and Yugoslavia this type of resistance is already recognized as a small slice of the total defense pie. In Norway, Denmark, France, West Germany, the Netherlands, Sweden, and Finland, limited government or semi-official studies, commission or committee reports, or parliamentary hearings on the policy have already been undertaken. Military, political and peace movement interest has been shown for some years in Austria. In some countries, notably the Netherlands, diverse political parties are already committed to the exploration of this national defense option.[1] The policy has already moved into the realm of practical politics and into the realm of the "thinkable" in the field of national security policies. For the most part, the question no longer is whether this policy has any relevance for the defense policies of diverse European governments and societies, but rather the question has become to what extent, when, and how this type of resistance should be incorporated into existing national policies.

This book aims to explain how and why civilian-based defense may work against attackers and to explore how it might be applied to prevent and defend against attacks on Western European countries more adequately than present policies. The volume will also suggest some next steps in considering this policy for meeting the deterrence and defense needs of those diverse countries. This book is intended to stimulate the exploration, consideration, and development of the policy beyond its present stage, not to be a substitute for the needed future work on its development. Blueprints ready for application to particular countries and crises will therefore not be found in this book, nor even plans for the needed preparations and training. Those necessarily await the kinds of studies recommended here. Much work is required to adapt the general policy to the needs and conditions of particular societies.

Let us then first explore briefly the kinds of security threats to Western European countries for which deterrence and defense policies are needed. The danger of a Soviet invasion of Western European countries, or the threat of such action to obtain internal political changes desired by the Soviet Union, is widely recognized as the most serious security threat. This volume does not depart from that judgment. However, it is not the only threat to the security of Western European countries, even at present. In addition to prominent treatment of the Soviet threat, attention will also be given to other threats. These include possible future aggression from as yet unknown sources and from internal usurpations, especially in the form of coup d'état. Therefore, even though an exclusive focus on the Soviet threat would considerably simplify the discussion, we shall attempt a more balanced consideration of Western European security problems.

Full agreement with this assessment of the security threats is not necessary in order for civilian-based defense to be seen as relevant for those countries. It is true that dangers are sometimes exaggerated or imagined by members of the general public, security analysts, and political leaders. It is also true, however, that real dangers often do exist and that other threats can arise which were not expected only a short time before. We can differ in our identification of the sources of threats to the countries of Western Europe and in our estimation of their gravity. Yet we can agree that the peoples of Europe should be able to ward off attacks and to protect themselves, their ways of life, and their liberties.

It is sometimes argued that the problem of invasions has been made obsolete by nuclear weapons. That is not the case, however. Invasions still occur in Europe and elsewhere. Conventional military invasions remain the classic threat for which deterrence and defense capacity is sought. The major preoccupation of NATO and non-aligned Western European defense planners is a Soviet conventional invasion and occupation of certain Western European countries. Nearly all other military considerations are, in their thinking, subordinate to, or derived from it. This is true especially of the NATO policy of "first use" of nuclear weapons: it is intended to counter a possible Soviet conventional invasion. That is why President Reagan's former national security adviser, William P. Clark, wrote in July 1982: "A pledge of no first use of nuclear weapons on the part of NATO could, in fact, lead the Soviets to believe that Western Europe was open to conventional aggression."[2]

While undoubtedly not all fears of the Soviet Union are justified, some are. It is no secret that the policies and actions of the Soviet Union have often fallen short of exemplary international behavior. Fears of a Soviet invasion may at times be exaggerated, but some Soviet military activities have been disturbing. The Soviet Union has used its military forces for political objectives in Eastern Europe since the end of the Second World War: first, to place Communist parties in power, and then to discourage and crush popular resistance against those systems. The Soviet Union has also established its military forces in Eastern Europe and led a military alliance with the Communist-ruled Eastern European states. All this has made many people wary of Soviet policy objectives.

The Soviet motives for invading and occupying countries in Western Europe could include placing local Communist parties in power, securing military bases or safer shipping and naval routes, gaining control of Western Europe's large industrial resources, or countering feared military or political developments in those countries.

Both those countries directly bordering the Soviet Union or Warsaw Treaty Organization members and other countries farther west therefore need the capacity to deter possible Soviet aggression and to defend successfully against it. That objective is expressed in the deterrence and defense policies of both aligned and non-aligned Western European countries. Despite variations in each Western European country as to the perceived extent of a Soviet military threat, each one has legitimate defense needs.

Even so, some people do not believe that a serious Soviet threat to Western Europe exists. These views take two forms. First, an impressive case can be made that the USSR already has too many serious internal problems and difficulties in controlling Eastern Europe to contemplate seriously invading and occupying much of Western Europe, even assuming that the Soviet leadership wished to do so. Second, other persons explain Soviet military preparations and actions as preventive or defensive responses to perceived United States and NATO military capacities and threats.

One can take the view that the Soviet Union might well invade Western European countries, or the view that there is no such threat. In either case, there are reasons to explore whether viable policies might be developed effectively to deter and defend against possible threats of invasion from any source and also internal usurpations, yet do so by means which could reduce the dangers to the survival of Europe posed by present nuclear policies.

Some European countries do not view the USSR as the primary threat; yet they still have defense needs that may derive from foreseeable threats from other neighbors, from existing internal forces, or from as yet unidentified future domestic or foreign dangers. Some countries may, for example, perceive an active threat from a neighboring state. For example, Greece has long been worried about the intentions of Turkey, especially in relation to the Greek population on Cyprus. European countries have in the past experienced invasions from a variety of states, including unexpected attacks from supposedly "friendly" ones. For example, few would have predicted in the early 1960s that Czechoslovakia, with its rigid Communist system, would be invaded by the Soviet Union and its Warsaw Treaty Organization allies before the end of the decade. The uncertainty of the sources of future international dangers must be built into calculations about defense and security problems and policies.

Recognition of the dangers of invasions and usurpations need not lead to desperation, paranoia, or escapist reactions. It is important to remember that not all feared and expected attacks actually occur. First of all, misperceptions may have created unjustified fears, and the intent to attack may never actually have been present. Second, although an attack may have been contemplated, various changes in the hostile state or in the international situation may have occurred, causing the hostile plans to be abandoned. Finally, and most importantly here, the deterrence and defense policies of the intended victim may have dissuaded or deterred the would-be attacker.

Some people minimize the need to develop a viable policy actually to defend Western European countries. They believe that this option has been superseded by the present nuclear weapons policies of each side. It is often believed that the emphasis must be placed instead on nuclear deterrence—not actual defense against conventional invasion. Such people are often convinced that plans which make escalation from defense efforts to nuclear war virtually inevitable are advantageous, because that will increase deterrence and hopefully prevent an invasion in the first place. It is the view of this book, however, that it is both too dangerous and unnecessary to link nuclear weapons to defense measures to deter invasions.

If invasions do occur in Europe, neither they nor defense against them need lead to the use of nuclear weapons. Viable defense is still needed against conventional invasions. Indeed, choosing very different security policies for Western European countries can make nuclear war far less likely.

It can be counterproductive for an invader to use nuclear weapons if the defenders and their allies do not have them. International aggression is usually launched to achieve certain objectives: territorial, political, economic, ideological, or military. Those objectives could well be made unrealizable by using nuclear weapons, due to the anticipated contamination by radioactivity and expected physical destruction and loss of life in the attacked country. Dead people are difficult to indoctrinate, and destroyed factories are unproductive. The use of nuclear weapons against a nonnuclear country being invaded would therefore be highly unlikely, unless that country is part of a nuclear alliance and is thought to provide military bases for its nuclear allies.

Use of nuclear weapons against an attacked country is far more likely, however, if it is a member of a nuclear alliance or has nuclear bases on its territory. The attacker may then use nuclear weapons either as (1) a pre-emptive attack to prevent a feared imminent nuclear attack, or (2) an escalation of a conventional military conflict to prevent defeat.

Choice of a very different, nonnuclear, dissuasion and defense policy can largely preclude a nuclear war initiated by a pre-emptive attack or by escalation from a defense struggle. A country without nuclear weapons, bases, or alliances is far less likely to be the victim of a pre-emptive strike than one with them. Escalation of a defense struggle to nuclear war is virtually impossible if the attacked country does not rely on conventional military weaponry and on nuclear war preparations or alliances. (This topic is discussed more fully in Chapter 6.) Policy options which exclude both conventional and nuclear weapons are, however, unacceptable to most people unless those options possess alternative realistic means to deter and defend against invasions.

Whether one is primarily concerned with effectively deterring and defeating invasions or with drastically reducing the chances of nuclear destruction of one's country, it is very important to explore all reasonable options in security policies. Internal take-overs are another security threat for which deterrence and defense capacity is required. These internal attacks usually take the form of coups d'état by military, right-wing, neo-fascist, Communist, or other groups.[3] These may be of purely internal origin or occur through foreign instigation of an internal group. However, internal attacks may also take the form of executive usurpations. Elected presidents or prime ministers may usurp power by declaring a state òf emergency, cancelling elections, and suspending civil liberties and constitutional procedures. Both types of take-overs are serious security threats against constitutional democracies because they may destroy the constitutional system, bring to power a dictatorial regime, and at times provoke serious international crises and foreign military intervention.

Since the Second World War, coups have occurred in Czechoslovakia (1948), Greece (several times), Cyprus, France (the 1961 Algiers generals' revolt), and Spain (1981). Some of these had significant impact on Western European security, even though not all were successful. The Cyprus coup in 1974 triggered the Turkish invasion and the subsequent division of Cyprus, and resulted in a major and enduring problem for NATO. There were repeated rumors of possible military take-overs in Italy in the 1970s, and fears of coups there remain. Much of the worry of constitutional democrats about Communist Party participation in coalition governments in France and Italy is rooted in the fear that Communist power-bases in the government could be used to facilitate a full Communist take-over, as in Czechoslovakia in 1948.

Despite the demonstrated dangers of coups d'état, the defense policies of most countries ignore this problem. This may be largely because the defense policies in Western European countries are exclusively or predominantly military ones, and there is no military answer to coups or executive usurpations short of the risk of civil war. This is because military defense against a military coup would require the population, with or without part of the military forces, to fight its own military forces conducting the coup. A coup by a political party or clique would require the military forces (if loyal) and population to fight against the political forces and their paramilitary units or supporters from the regular police and military forces.

Foreign attacks may take forms other than conventional invasions and support of coups d'état, such as conventional bombings and chemical, biological, and nuclear attacks. Each of these, as with all other possible forms of attack, merits separate detailed analyses of its characteristics, conditions, likelihood, and of possible defensive countermeasures. These forms of military attack are far more likely in a conflict in which both sides are prepared to use them, either as a first strike or in retaliation. Such bombings or attacks may also occur by previously unintended escalation during a massive conventional war or as deliberate measures to prevent defeat. Bombings, or chemical, biological, and nuclear attacks, however, may be far less likely to occur outside the context of a major war, being especially unlikely in the ·face of a nonmilitary defense against conventional invasions.

PROBLEMS OF PRESENT POLICIES

For many years the security and defense policies for Western Europe seemed to most people to be settled and working well. No war had broken out between the Eastern and Western blocs. For a time—with the easing of tensions between the two Germanies, détente, the Helsinki agreement, and the settling of frontiers—old dangers even seemed to be receding. Despite the dangers and costs of established policies, few saw reason in the new climate of optimism to look in fresh directions for new deterrence and defense policies.

The grounds for optimism have faded. The increase in political tensions between the United States and the Soviet Union is only a part of the shift. The escalation of the military build-up on both sides is more serious. In this situation, some people have become convinced that present Western policies are too weak and others that the dangers of nuclear war are too severe.

In recent years significant changes in public attitudes toward Western security policies have occurred. First, more people are aware of the dangers to Europeans posed by the deployment of American and Soviet nuclear weapons and their delivery systems. People understandably worry about the consequences of these in case of war. In this situation, many Europeans have become skeptical of the Soviet threat, or of the American commitment to Europe, or of both. They are also convinced that both the U.S. and the USSR may be prepared to destroy Europe to gain their own objectives. They may, for example, be willing to wage nuclear war provided they believe it can be limited to Europe. That prospect does nothing to convince Europeans that present policies are satisfactory.

Second, modern military technology, especially conventional weaponry, is extremely expensive. This places economies under additional stress at times of serious economic difficulties. Consequently, the domestic political or economic needs and problems of individual countries may be seen as legitimate competitors for military expenditures; they may even receive priority over stated defense needs and alliance obligations.

Third, an awareness seems to have gradually come that all the military might of the United States and the Atlantic Alliance is useless for assisting the peoples of Eastern Europe to cast off their Soviet-backed Communist rulers. Given the political stance of NATO and the political rhetoric that often accompanies pleas for increased appropriations for meeting Western European security needs, that is a remarkable incapacity.

Thus, with time, several fundamental problems of the established security policies have begun to emerge. In the following section we will focus primarily on two of these: the dangers of nuclear war and the limitations on military means to achieve liberation. The first of these must be seen in the context of the objectives of increasing the security of the peoples of Western Europe.

Nuclear deterrence theory has had considerable appeal. All countries prefer not to be attacked in the first place, thereby avoiding the need for actual defense struggles, and also the aid of a powerful ally is often a comfort. While the actual use of nuclear weapons would be disastrous, it has been believed that their role as a threat would prevent both aggression and war. It has consequently been believed that steps which tie international aggression to the possibility or probability of nuclear responses are advantageous because they will deter aggression or, if not, defeat it.

NATO policy makers and their supporters minimize the dangers of nuclear weapons and concentrate on their supposed positive achievement—deterring attack—and their supposed positive potential—halting a Soviet conventional invasion. If restrictively applied against advancing Soviet forces, they argue in effect, these weapons will create a nuclear moat to prevent a Soviet scaling of the Western European castle walls. Concentration on that optimistic interpretation helps us to avoid facing the dangers of nuclear deterrence for the actual defense of Europe. It ignores the policy's weaknesses, destabilizing shifts in military strengths, and the constant development of refined and new weapons, delivery systems, and counter-weapons, and in war the likely annihilating consequences. All these strongly increase the destructiveness of future war and prevent effective stabilization and arms control.

Rather than concentrating primarily on the optimistic view of present policies, we need to face the fundamental difficulties with Western European defense and security policies. These are revealed by addressing basic questions. Can NATO actually protect Europe, and if so, how? What are the aims of NATO military policy? Obviously, one is deterrence against Soviet attack, but by what means and with what risks? Another is defense, but is defense compatible with the chosen means of deterrence? Does deterrence always succeed? Is dependence on others for one's own defense acceptable in light of past experience and the uncertainties of the future?

The grand strategy of the North Atlantic Treaty Organization is based on the assumption that Western European countries could not, individually or collectively, successfully defend themselves against an all-out Soviet conventional invasion without U.S. nuclear assistance. That assumption, if true, leads to acceptance of dependence on the United States. The assumption, further, is that even with U.S. help, conventional military defense measures for Europe would probably fail. That has been the policy assumption of both NATO and the United States (although some people challenge its validity). The NATO alliance therefore believes it requires U.S. nuclear weapons to deter or to defeat possible attack.

This assumption has underpinned U.S. and NATO plans for decades, from the time of John Foster Dulles' doctrine of "massive retaliation" to today's tactical nuclear weapons, neutron bombs, and Pershing II and cruise missiles. This assumption immediately creates a dependence on nuclear weapons. It shifts attention from the capacity to defend (and to deter by a perceived ability to defend successfully) to the capacity to deter by an ability to inflict massive destruction. There appears to have been no serious search by NATO for other means of defense and deterrence outside conventional military and nuclear options.

Indeed, such a search has usually been presumed to be unnecessary, and the strong chance that nuclear war would result from resistance to invasion was seen to be beneficial. This view was argued in early 1982 by General Bernard Rogers, Supreme Allied Commander in Europe of NATO. He indicated that in conventional military terms Warsaw Pact forces were superior to those of NATO: "The approximate static balances in some key areas are: 2:1 against NATO in divisions, 2.5:1 against NATO in tanks in theater, and 3:1 against NATO in artillery pieces." He also maintained that the trend was "towards a widening of the current imbalance in force capabilities," producing a gap which "gets wider every year." Consequently, he stressed a build-up of both conventional and nuclear deterrence capacities, closely tied together:

> The basis of NATO's military planning is security through credible deterrence. There must be clearly perceived linkages among conventional, theater, and strategic nuclear legs in NATO's triad of forces in order to maintain an incalculable risk for any aggressor. Should aggression occur, the Alliance would conduct a forward defense of NATO territory, responding as necessary with direct defense, deliberate escalation, and general nuclear release, to keep the level of violence consistent with maintaining the territorial integrity of all NATO members. NATO thus seeks to induce the enemy to make the *political* decision to cease aggression and withdraw, even though he still possesses the military capabilities to continue.[4] (Emphasis in the original)

This deliberate intertwining of conventional and nuclear responses, of nuclear deterrence and combat strategies, and of conventional "direct defense" with "deliberate escalation, and general nuclear release" creates a remarkable situation. To expect that this strategy in combat could maintain "the territorial integrity of all NATO members" in any sense related to genuine defense of the peoples of those countries is highly questionable.

Clearly, the gravest weakness of the present nuclear deterrence policy is that it can fail, producing a catastrophe. No system of deterrence can ever be guaranteed to deter. In 1959 Bernard Brodie, a prominent early nuclear weapons analyst, wrote that the strategy of deterrence "ought always to envisage the possibility of deterrence failing."[5] "Of course," wrote Glenn Snyder (another analyst of that period) "the primary objective in dealing with the threat of all-out attack is to deter it. But we can never have absolute confidence in deterrence. . . . "[6]

It is therefore necessary that the consequences of the failure of any deterrence system not be catastrophic. Remedial means capable of defending the attacked society must be ready for operation. While it is arguable that nuclear capacities may significantly reduce the chances of a country being attacked, the possibility is not eliminated, and may even be increased. Attack may still occur deliberately (as a pre-emptive strike or the result of an escalating conflict) or following unintended or accidental events. In the case of large-scale use of nuclear weapons, the failure of deterrence would be catastrophic, and there could be no adequate remedial measures or effective defense. This is especially true in the densely populated countries of Western Europe.

NATO plans include the use of various types of smaller nuclear weapons in Western Europe itself against invading Soviet forces. This is an indication that NATO planners have become so involved in the available military hardware they have lost sight of the objective: the defense of the Europeans and their societies. Major use of nuclear weapons in Europe would destroy the very people supposedly being "defended." Many people in NATO countries fear that such use of nuclear weapons would initiate a radioactive duel—something very different from defense—bordered only by the Atlantic and the Vistula. NATO strategists may argue that the planned use of nuclear weapons against Soviet forces is intended to strengthen deterrence so as to prevent an invasion in the first place. However, since deterrence can fail, when the nuclear weapons are actually used against an invasion, they would destroy the people the policy was supposed to protect. That casts doubt on the good sense (and perhaps even the credibility) of such a policy, even for deterrence alone.

Present NATO strategies that depend on threat or use of nuclear weapons suffer from several additional serious problems. It has been widely assumed, for instance, that a country possessing nuclear weapons, or basing those of an ally on its soil, will have gained increased safety from nuclear attack. The opposite may be true, as noted above. A country which directly possesses nuclear weapons, or provides bases for them, or even belongs to a nuclear alliance (hence causing suspicion of regular or emergency basing), makes it virtually inevitable that other, potentially hostile, nuclear powers will target it. This is because, whatever one's actual intent, any of those steps will be seen as extremely dangerous by potential opponents.

Such a country will be seen as a potential attacker or accomplice to a nuclear attack, either by pre-emptive strike or by escalation of a conventional war. Powers feeling threatened will then respond by targeting the potential attacker. Adoption or basing of nuclear weapons by any country thereby immensely multiplies the dangers which face it. Overwhelmingly, it is the nuclear powers which fear attack, not the countries with no nuclear capacities or bases. This in part explains why many Europeans oppose deployment of nuclear weapons on their soil.

NATO's reliance on nuclear weapons to achieve security for Western Europe contributes to serious instability. This policy and its assumptions create very strong and seemingly uncontrollable pressures to equal, counter, and supersede the technology of the other side. It becomes more complex as the number of nuclear powers grows, but it is very serious even when the United States and the Soviet Union are in a class of their own. Whatever the original objective, both refinements in existing technologies and development of new ones bring increased insecurity. Research and development programs in this field and measures to "modernize" existing weaponry to make deterrence "more credible" are part of this process. There is no end to these pressures within the framework of military assumptions.

Another problem of the nuclear deterrence policy is that possession of nuclear weapons by any state contributes to their proliferation to others, regardless of what that state may do to prevent their spread. This is especially true of the continued possession and development of nuclear weapons on a massive scale by the superpowers. The possession of this weaponry demonstrates the belief of those governments in its utility for their own purposes—deterrence, threats, attack, retaliation, defense, prestige, influence, or leverage. Leaders of other states also have those motives. The superpowers' continued nuclear policies undermine the credibility of their officials' political moralizing and diplomatic pressuring for nonproliferation. Even though at present proliferation is significantly more likely outside of Europe, such developments will contribute to increasing international instability and the dangers of nuclear war, which might even involve Europe directly.

The nuclear deterrent approach suffers an additional serious political problem. It completely lacks any means to undermine a hostile foreign dictatorial system—one that oppresses people at home and may also threaten international aggression. In fact, political stability comes to be seen as a major contributing factor in preventing nuclear war. The nuclear deterrence policy thus contributes to maintenance of the political status quo. The policy lacks capability either to help undermine tyranny or to abolish the foreign threat to the liberty and survival of one's own country. For example, the combination of the extremely destructive character of modern military weapons and the alliance structures in Eastern and Western Europe actually bolsters Soviet hegemony. That combination leaves Eastern Europe under Soviet control and increases Soviet reasons to repress liberation movements among its Warsaw Pact allies. They must not be allowed to defect out of the alliance.

Nor can the vast NATO military power be used to assist the peoples of Eastern Europe. The military and alliance situation prohibits Western military assistance to liberation movements there, even at times of massive popular uprisings and resistance against the Communist regimes or Soviet interventions (as in East Germany in 1953, Hungary in 1956, Czechoslovakia in 1968, or Poland since 1980) because military assistance would risk massive conventional and even nuclear war. No capability exists in present military policies to assist the self-liberation of the peoples of Eastern Europe. Nor is that weakness balanced by any compensating ability to reduce international tensions and establish greater trust and security.

Furthermore, the relationships within the NATO alliance are not totally satisfactory for its own members. In the long run, the dependence of Western European countries on the United States for their collective deterrence and defense, and in some cases even for their individual defense policies, tends to be seen by all parties as unsatisfactory. Resentments may build up on both sides, and European countries may seek alternative paths. France, for example, has developed its own nuclear weapons along with its conventional forces and withdrawn from NATO activities. Despite the Soviet Union's record, some Western European countries might seek a closer diplomatic and economic relationship with it while weakening their reliance on NATO or even withdrawing from the alliance. In other cases, dependence on the U.S.—combined with distrust of its intentions, judgment, or capabilities—may contribute to strong popular pressures to break with NATO before developing viable alternative defense policies.

The dependence relationship also has high costs for the United States. The U.S. consistently has spent the highest percentage of total NATO outlay—57 to 62 percent during 1969–1979. The U.S. also had the highest military expenditure as a percentage of the gross national product of any NATO member—6.28 percent for the U.S. during the decade 1969 to 1978, while the average for the European NATO members during that decade ranged from 3.6 to 3.9 percent. The U.S. expenditures of course include non-NATO costs.[7]

Estimates made in 1979 of the annual costs to the U.S. of just the NATO commitment varied from $20,000,000,000 to $50,000,000,000.[8] On July 20, 1984 'The New York Times' reported far higher costs. Richard Halloran reported that confidential assessments of military spending made separately by the U.S. Department of Defense and the General Accounting Office, an investigative agency of Congress, showed that more than half of the U.S. military budget was spent on efforts to provide security and defense for Western Europe. The Pentagon assessment—'United States Expenditures in Support of NATO'—showed that for fiscal year 1985, beginning October 1, 1984, 58 percent of the U.S. military budget was allocated for the defense of other members of NATO.

The 'New York Times' article quoted that report as saying that "the total cost of European-deployed United States forces and all of the United States forces that we have pledged to contribute as NATO reinforcements over the course of a conflict" totalled $177,000,000,000, or over three-and-a-half times the higher 1979 estimate. That was over 58 percent of President Reagan's initial military budget request of $306,000,000,000. (The report also argued that this total could be misleading, and various items should not actually be included.)

The General Accounting Office report used figures from fiscal year 1982. It stated that that year 56 percent of U.S. military expenditures went to U.S. forces in Europe or in the U.S. available for use in Europe in case of a war. Based on slightly different calculations (including reinforcements and a share of the strategic nuclear forces), the GAO report stated that in 1982 $122,000,000,000 of the U.S. military budget was committed to NATO. Halloran cited figures from the International Institute of Strategic Studies in London to the effect that in 1983 Americans paid 10 percent of their per capita income on military expenditures while the proportion for Europeans was only one-third as much.[9]

Such immense expenditures obviously must have an economic, social, and political impact on the other policies of the United States. That is to say nothing of the consequences of such expenditures on the country's national debt. For example, the Pentagon estimate of $177,000,000,000 as the cost of the United States commitment to NATO for fiscal year 1985 should be compared to the Office of Management and Budget projection of a budget deficit of $172,400,000,000 for the 1985 fiscal year. The Congressional Budget Office projection was a deficit of $178,000,000,000.[10] For fiscal year 1986, the federal budget was expected to show a deficit of $180,000,000,000.[11] This means that approximately the entire U.S. budget deficit for these years would not exist if European NATO members were self-reliant in their defense policies.

U.S. pressures on its allies to increase their share of NATO's military expenditures and forces have in the past produced resentments and exacerbated existing strains within the alliance. This is at least in part because military weaponry and forces are intrinsically extremely expensive, and because the acceptance of full responsibility for them by the European countries would have significant social, economic, and political consequences, often producing unwanted problems.

Two additional major difficulties with present Western European security policies exist. First, greater fear of nuclear annihilation than of Soviet occupation, combined with the perceived absence of a third option, could lead almost any NATO member in Europe to capitulate in an extreme crisis, somewhat as Denmark did in 1940 in the face of certain military defeat. That prospect seriously weakens the credibility of nuclear deterrence. Capitulation is not, of course, the only option in such a case: paramilitary and nonmilitary resistance would remain possible alternatives. Despite that, no significant plans exist—either in NATO as a whole or in individual member countries—to continue the defense effort by either guerrilla or non-violent struggle against foreign occupations.

Government surrender without preparations for other resistance would leave the population with no guidance for continuing defense struggle. The people would lack even such basic resources as handbooks on how to resist foreign occupation, prepared communication equipment, and financial resources. Lack of preparations to help ensure strong continuing popular resistance would make submission to occupation rule more likely; the prospect of easy occupation rule could itself in certain situations contribute to a decision to invade.

Second, the known dangers of nuclear weapons have already fuelled significant popular protest and resistance movements against them, the policies of which they are a part, and the NATO alliance itself. This was shown by the mass demonstrations in various European countries during the early 1980s. Such opposition movements may result in government decisions which weaken military preparations and alliance policies without replacing them with viable alternative ways of addressing genuine defense needs and security threats by less dangerous means. Such an accusation is sometimes levelled at the British peace movements of the 1930s.

The basic problems of the NATO nuclear deterrence strategy surveyed above are longstanding. The substantive weaknesses of that policy underlie the unease, concern, and outright disaffection which has surfaced in various Western European countries among people with widely differing beliefs. Relatively minor adjustments in that policy cannot correct its basic weaknesses.

A CONVENTIONAL MILITARY SOLUTION?

With deterrence and defense by nuclear weapons extremely perilous, various people have sought ways to reduce the danger. One proposal recommends that NATO undertake a major increase in its conventional military capacity. The reasoning is that if conventional military means could become more powerful, thereby playing a significantly greater role in deterring and defending against a Soviet conventional military attack, the need for a deliberate resort to nuclear weapons could be reduced.

Even now, not everyone is convinced that NATO's conventional forces are as clearly inferior to those of the Soviet Union as General Rogers has suggested. For example, John J. Mearsheimer has argued that "NATO is in relatively good shape on the conventional level" and that "the balance of conventional forces is nowhere near as unfavorable as it is so often portrayed to be." [12] His claim is not, however, very extreme:

> Certainly NATO does not have the capacity to *win* a conventional war on the continent against the Soviets. NATO does have, however, the wherewithal to *deny* the Soviets a quick victory and then to turn the conflict into a lengthy war of attrition, where NATO's advantage in population and GNP would not bode well for the Soviets. [13] (Emphases in the original)

In terms of the defense of the peoples of Western and Eastern Europe, however, that prospect is not an optimistic forecast. It offers only a distant chance of victory, the prospect of massive destruction and death by conventional military means—some analysts suggest this would approach nuclear levels [14] — and the constant risk of escalation to nuclear war.

Others, such as 'The Economist' in London, have argued that although NATO's present conventional military forces could not successfully defeat a Soviet conventional sweep westward, they could do so given major increases in military hardware, personnel, mobilization capacity, war production preparations, and anti-submarine forces. Even then, these analysts project a long war, with a remaining possibility of nuclear escalation. [15] (Barring that development, it should be recalled that even the military technology of the 1940s was sufficient to destroy large areas of Europe.) Even if a conventional NATO build-up were judged desirable, there would be serious political difficulties in achieving it in both Western Europe and the United States, due to the high economic and political costs. Without a perceived alternative, this political constraint supports the current NATO reliance on nuclear weapons.

Whatever spokesmen may say, justifications of nuclear weapons as key parts of NATO's strategic responses to conventional attacks are unmistakably rooted in the perceived weaknesses of conventional military forces alone for deterrence and defense in Western Europe. These inadequacies underlie the United States' refusal to make a pledge of "no first use" of nuclear weapons in a European conflict. Calls for "no first use" are weakened seriously unless they convince people and policy makers that some alternative to nuclear weapons can deter and defeat a Soviet conventional invasion. (McGeorge Bundy, George Kennan, Robert McNamara, and Gerard Smith in the

Spring 1982 issue of 'Foreign Affairs' therefore called for a prior strengthening of NATO conventional military forces in Europe.[16]) The exaggeration in former Secretary of State Alexander Haig's response to that article should not blind us to the necessity of a substantive alternative deterrence and defense capacity. Haig declared:

> Those in the West who advocate the adoption of a "no first use" policy seldom go on to propose that the United States reintroduce the draft, triple the size of its armed forces, and put its economy on a wartime footing. Yet in the absence of such steps, a pledge of "no first use" effectively leaves the West nothing with which to counterbalance the Soviet conventional advantages and geopolitical position in Europe.[17]

Some concerned analysts, aware of the dangers both of use of nuclear weapons to repel a Soviet conventional invasion and of weakness in face of the Soviet threat, have proposed a major increase in NATO's conventional military capacity. This was recommended by the European Security Study, 'Strengthening Conventional Deterrence in Europe: Proposals for the 1980s', prepared by a Steering Group of 26 distinguished Americans and Europeans under the auspices of the American Academy of Arts and Sciences. As an important study, sincerely attempting to deal with difficult problems, it merits some detailed attention to determine the adequacy of its recommendations.

The Study examined how NATO could improve its conventional military capacity so as to enhance its deterrence of Soviet aggression and yet lessen its dependence on possible early use of nuclear weapons. The Study assumed that NATO would continue to require nuclear weapons for possible later stages of such a conflict and also for deterrence. While the Study stated that "the Soviet Union's challenge to NATO and its peoples is at present primarily political," there was no consideration of political ways of meeting that political challenge.[18] The means considered were exclusively military.

Every effort to reduce the chances of nuclear war is admirable, and it is possible that the recommendations of the European Security Study might contribute to that reduction to some degree. However, the Study's conclusions are not very reassuring. They do not offer a fundamental reconsideration of ways to provide security for Western Europe.

The Study recommends developing a conventional military capacity adequate for deterring and defeating a Soviet conventional military invasion. This is to be done primarily by developing and adopting new technologies for conventional weapons and delivery systems with superior targeting capabilities and by improving ways to use existing conventional forces and those now under procurement.

As a consequence, the Study continues, NATO should be able to reduce or eliminate use of nuclear weapons in "tactical missions in support of NATO forward defenses" or in destroying Warsaw Treaty Organization air power. It could also "reduce its reliance on possible early use of nuclear weapons to defeat Warsaw Pact forces" as they attempt to penetrate NATO forward defenses. All this is to be achieved at a probable cost of $20,000,000,000.

Although the proposed shifts in weaponry may "raise the nuclear threshold," grave dangers will continue. The recommendations of the Study do not provide a solution to the basic problem of Western European security, i.e., the means adopted to provide that security may contribute directly to the massive destruction of those very societies. The authors report that the present and new conventional military weaponry could produce a war significantly more destructive than the Second World War. The Study emphasizes that in that situation NATO's conventional "forces themselves and the NATO infrastructure must be sufficiently resilient, redundant, and survivable to withstand the shock of modern war at a level heretofore not experienced in Europe, and to maintain essential operations," specifically to perform five named military missions.[19] That is, the task of the military, then, must be to defend the military so that it can continue combat operations.

No mention is made, however, of the effects of such a war on the civilian population and the society being "defended." That is very disappointing, since the authors themselves earlier stated the precept that "all forms of military strength . . . must be designed and deployed in such a fashion that they do in fact deter and defend."[20] With such capable members of the Study's Steering Group, it is most unlikely that a gap existed in either their memory or their analytical capacity. It is much more probable that these men could not find means which "do in fact deter and defend" within the context of "forms of military strength."

That is not, however, the end of the weaknesses of this Study. Even taking the claims of the authors at face value, if all their proposals are implemented, the danger of nuclear war still remains: "Moreover, given the existence of nuclear weapons, we recognize that any armed conflict in Europe entails a risk of becoming nuclear."[21]

We are justified in continuing to search for a policy less likely to contribute to the defeat of its own objectives, one which will not result in annihilation in place of defense. That search needs to be pursued with new vigor. Recognizing significant problems with present defense and security policies can lead to an atmosphere of intellectual ferment, which may yield innovative thinking. It is time to begin this new thinking, for it can contribute to discovery or development of alternative solutions to Western Europe's security problems.

THE NEED FOR INNOVATIVE THINKING

Some people may doubt that all the problems attributed above to present NATO policies exist or are as serious as suggested. Still more may grant that such problems exist but believe that they are at least equalled in gravity by new ones which would arise if NATO's nuclear capacity were abandoned. Yet very few people indeed would argue that the present policies to ensure security and protection for Western Europe are so perfect that other options should not even be investigated. They know that to resist even the exploration of new security options means a willingness to live forever with the risks of nuclear war or the dangers of domination in Europe.

Investigation of possible new policies is also justified by the need to meet the security problems of coming decades. Clearly, those may take new forms which cannot be fully anticipated. Past changes in military technology, means of communication, psychological manipulation, and population control do not induce optimism about the future internal and external threats to political freedom. This is especially true in the context of the accelerating tendencies for even non-malevolent governments to be controlled by small élites, rather than by a participating citizenry. There are also signs that increased economic interdependence and political integration may provide new means of control and domination and enlarged military power. Therefore, it is important to explore new means providing effective defense against both older and newer types of attack and domination.

Despite the gravity of present and future security problems, remarkably little innovative thinking has occurred. Two of the factors which help explain the paucity of innovative thinking in this field have been discussed above, in the section on the problems of present policies. Supporters of present security policies have concentrated on their supposed positive achievements, while critics of those policies have neglected genuine defense and security problems.

Another important reason is that military strategies which can ensure protection of the civilian population at home are non-existent. The myth continues that military forces can actually defend the country at the frontiers, preventing with certainty the intrusion of enemy weapons and forces by air or land. However, that possibility was destroyed long ago by the introduction of the airplane and, to a lesser degree, of the tank, as well as more recently of the atomic bomb and the long-range rocket. These weapons can fly over the frontier or smash through it, making effective defense at the frontiers impossible. Recognition of that drastic change should have led to exploration of other ways to prevent destructive attacks on the civilian society and to make them inappropriate or even counterproductive for achieving the attackers' political, economic, ideological, or other objectives.

However, policy makers—unable to provide defense—instead pursued the quest for yet more destructive forms of offensive military technology. This found justification in the old doctrine that offense is the best form of defense. The doctrine that the strong, capable of defending themselves, are less likely to be attacked than the weak, became the very different doctrine of nuclear deterrence. In it, the capacity to defend in order to deter has been replaced by the capability to destroy massively without the ability to defend.

Other factors have also helped to shift attention from the meaning and primacy of defense. These include the utilization of military forces for offensive purposes, for establishing or bolstering domestic political control and domination, and for gaining or wielding international "influence." None of these is necessarily tied to effective defense, strictly defined—protection, preservation, and the warding off of danger. Yet these other uses of military forces have provided different justifications for military systems, and distracted attention from the vital task of defense.

Finally, a longstanding and massive transoceanic confusion about the basic concepts used in strategic thinking also helps explain the lack of fundamental innovation in European security policies. Quite distinct concepts, such as "defense," "deterrence," "security," and "military," have been used imprecisely and even interchangeably. The old United States "Department of War" has become the "Department of Defense" at the very time when defense itself has become impossible by military means. Inadequate care has been given to consideration of how particular projected weapons and strategies are to contribute causally to the actual security and defense of the people whose country might be attacked—that is, to the traditional conception of national defense. Even peace groups, to their own detriment, have passively accepted this distorting political parlance and from anti-war and anti-military motives have opposed "defense appropriations" and "defense preparations"—when virtually no one wants to be defenseless. This conceptual confusion has resulted in an inability to think clearly or even to see the need to consider alternative policies.

CLARIFICATION OF BASIC CONCEPTS

"Defense," "military weaponry," "deterrence," and "destructive capacity" are by no means identical, and may even be incompatible with one another. Let us first distinguish between "defense" and "military." The term "defense" is rarely carefully used. The U.S. 'Department of Defense Dictionary of Military and Associated Terms', issued by the Joint Chiefs of Staff, for example, does not even contain a definition of "defense" or "national defense."[22]

"Defense" is used here to mean the protection or preservation of a country's independence, its right to choose its own way of life, institutions, and standards of legitimacy, and the protection of its own people's lives, freedom, and opportunities for future development. "Defense" may also be defined as instrumentally effective action to defend—that is, action which preserves, wards off, protects and minimizes harm in the face of hostile attack.[23] Such actions as invading or bombing another country, or arranging a coup d'état against its government, would not be "defense" but "attack" and would constitute international aggression.

Military means have been recognized throughout history as the predominant methods used to provide defense. However, defense and military means are not synonymous. In certain situations military means have been incapable of actually defending, as distinct from attacking or retaliating. This may have happened because the military means were too weak to repel the attack, because they were too strong and could bring only mutual destruction, or because it was impossible by any means to prevent intrusion of the attackers' weapons or military units. Military action by the attacked country may lead to defeat or bombardment of the aggressor country; but modern technology makes it impossible to protect the attacked home population, system, cities, and territory from destruction. On the other hand, as will be shown in later chapters, defense has sometimes been provided by improvised nonmilitary struggle.

"Defense" and "military," therefore, differ both conceptually and in practice. Defense denotes the objective outlined above, or means which actually produce that objective. Military capacity is only one set of means which may be intended to achieve the objective of defense; it may sometimes prove incapable of doing so (whatever else it may do).

It is, of course, desirable not to be attacked in the first place. To prevent attack, various influences and measures may be applied with the intent of dissuading attackers. "Dissuasion" here is conceived as the result of acts or processes which induce an opponent not to carry out a contemplated hostile action. Rational argument, moral appeal, increased cooperation, improved human understanding, distraction, adoption of a non-offensive policy, and deterrence may all be used to achieve dissuasion.

Current discussions usually ignore means of dissuasion other than deterrence, and sometimes even assume not only that deterrence must be military but also nuclear. "Deterrence," however, is a broader concept than military or nuclear deterrence. It is a particular type of dissuasion process which convinces potential attackers not to commit an aggressive or hostile act because certain consequences would follow which they would prefer to avoid. Violent means are not the only ones which can produce that punishment capacity. It can also be achieved by the ability to deny something the potential attacker needs, or seriously desires, or by producing other unacceptable consequences for the attacker. For example, the likely severance of necessary supplies of energy, materials, or markets, or denial of political, economic, or other objectives might force a potential invader to reconsider the contemplated aggression.

NATO policies, and those of individual countries in Western Europe, are based on the assumption that it is possible to deter a conventional military invasion only by strong conventional military preparations, weapons of mass destruction, or a combination of these. Those are not the only possibilities, however.

At times, deterrence against aggression might be provided by prepared capacity of the population to resist strongly (by violent or nonviolent means) the military occupation which usually follows an invasion. The prospect of an endless struggle in the occupied country—with high political and economic costs, without compensating gains—might produce effective deterrence. It might also be produced by the prospect of significant opposition—or even rebellion—at home and disaffection—or even mutiny—among the occupation troops. Those consequences are in most cases unlikely in face of military defense because the killing of the invading country's young men arouses most of its population in support of its military forces. However, in face of struggle by nonviolent means, in which lives are not threatened, it is easier for the attackers' population to see their home regime as oppressive and its aggression and repression as unjustified.

Deterrence might also be achieved by a credible threat by third parties with the required degree of solidarity to impose intolerable economic sanctions in the event of attack. These economic sanctions could take the form of a specific embargo (oil, for example), or of more comprehensive financial or trade disruption. Defense, dissuasion, and even deterrence, therefore, are not necessarily tied to military means, let alone to nuclear weapons.

Outside the nuclear context, deterrence and defense have been largely provided by the same capacities. The ability to defend successfully would also deter attacks. The separation of deterrence and defense has been predominantly due to the development of weapons of mass destruction.[24] The new weapons were capable of inflicting immense destruction, but were unable actually to defend.

The terms "security" and "national security" are also widely used in American discussions of deterrence and defense and of the dangers of international attack and aggression. These terms can obfuscate important issues if they are used without care. The terms are at times used, for example, in efforts to justify particular weapons, strategies, or policies, and even suppression of information and violations of civil liberties, without further explanation or evaluation why such steps are required. Since no one actively favors "national insecurity," the plea of a security requirement often goes unexamined. The nature of the presumed danger and the adequacy and appropriateness of the proposed remedy go unevaluated.

"Security" is used here to mean a condition of safety from military attack: "national security" is then the condition in which a nation or country is safe from military attack.

National security, as viewed here, is thus not identified, as it is in some U.S. policy circles, with the ability to secure from other parts of the world desired economic resources on one's own terms. Nor is it the same as capability to control the economic policies, political systems, and military actions of other countries and to intervene militarily throughout the world. Indeed, those aims are more related to domination than to security. In the long run, they are likely to produce hostile reactions toward, and therefore sometimes insecurity for, the country which has attempted to play that world role.

The plea of "national security" to justify internal repression and violation of civil liberties is also inconsistent with the usage recommended here. On the contrary, such measures are political attacks on the nation's security under a democratic constitutional system.

National security may exist because there are no dangers, but that situation is rare in the modern world. It is more likely to be the result of dissuasion of potential attackers. For example, it can result from deterrence of some sort; while still hostile, the potential attackers wish to avoid the consequences of aggression. The present situation—in which both the United States and the Soviet Union are prepared to launch massive destruction and death on the other within minutes without the possibility of effective protection in the attacked country—cannot be described as "national security." It is national and international insecurity.

When national security is violated with actual attack by conventional weapons, effective means are required to defend against the attack and to protect the citizenry in the best way possible. The defense objective is then to end the assault and restore the society's independence of action and condition of safety.

The choice of means to do this is highly important. Although some means intended to defend may instead threaten massive destruction, other forms may provide maximum defensive capacity with minimal injury to the country and its people. In addition to the means of defense, other measures and policies may contribute to national security by helping to dissuade potential attackers, or by increasing the internal resilience of the society which would increase its defense motivation and capacity.

SEEKING A NEW POLICY

Since deterrence of any kind can fail and use of nuclear weapons brings catastrophe, the peoples of Europe need another less dangerous way to deter and defend, so as to permit their independence and ways of life to continue. The defense of the European countries can and should be primarily their own responsibility. Therefore, they ought persistently to seek to develop alternative means of deterrence and defense by which in face of attack they could self-reliantly avoid not only capitulation but also holocaust by either conventional or nuclear means.

In seeking effective policies for deterrence and defense for Western Europe we are not restricted to present policies nor even to military ones. There is a wide range of possible options which might be proposed to meet Western European security needs more adequately, either as adjuncts or alternatives to current capabilities. These include build-up of diverse types of nuclear weapons and delivery systems; reassessment of chemical warfare policies in light of Soviet developments in that field; Mutual Balanced Force Reduction proposals; resurrection of the massive retaliation doctrine; territorial defense capacities involving indigenous guerrilla and sabotage preparations or precision guided weapons; major build-up of conventional military capacities; and civilian-based defense. These proposals differ in many respects, most notably in the extent to which they are intended to be preventive or actually defensive, and to which they risk massive destruction and killing of the peoples of Europe.

Our concern here is to provide deterrence and defense for Western European countries by means which produce maximum security and minimum destruction and loss of life, and which also have beneficial long-term consequences for the peoples of Europe. Most of the above proposals are therefore unsuitable, and several would even make the situation worse. Instead, we need to examine whether defense and security policies exist or can be developed which can effectively provide both capacities for deterrence and other forms of dissuasion and also capacities for actual defense, without prior acceptance of the doctrine that offense is superior to defense, or the assumptions of nuclear deterrence, or even of the framework of military technology.

We also need to examine the available policies which aim to provide a defensive capacity, and through it deterrence capability. The three basic defensive postures are: conventional military strength for defense only, guerrilla war capability for defense, and civilian-based defense. These may be applied singly or in combinations.[25] Our focus is on civilian-based defense. Although it is the least studied, it may turn out to have the most fundamental and beneficial consequences for the security problems of Western Europe.

2 CIVILIAN-BASED DEFENSE FOR WESTERN EUROPE?

IMPROVISED PROTOTYPE STRUGGLES AGAINST COUPS

In several cases, civilian struggle by noncooperation and defiance has been improvised against coups d'état and foreign aggression, as cited in the first chapter. Four of these cases will be described briefly here. The first two are of resistance against coups, in Germany in 1920 and in France in 1961. The next two cases are of resistance to foreign invasion and occupation, German resistance in the Ruhr in 1923 and Czechoslovak defense in 1968–1969.

These cases of popular and institutional noncooperation and defiance have their weaknesses, which is not surprising considering the complete absence of preparations and training. However, the struggles demonstrate that national defense by these unorthodox means has roots in political experience, and they illustrate some ways this policy can be applied against actual attacks.

The cases against coups are very different from each other. They both show, however, that a legitimated government may be saved by action of ordinary people, civil servants, or conscript soldiers, acting nonviolently to preserve the legal government.

Germany, 1920: In 1920 Germany's new Weimar Republic, already facing very severe problems, was attacked by a coup d'état organized by Dr. Wolfgang Kapp and Lieutenant-General Walter von Lüttwitz, with the backing of General Ludendorff. While most of the German army remained "neutral"—neither participating in nor opposing the coup—ex-soldiers organized in 'Freikorps' units of the Baltic Brigades occupied Berlin on March 12. The legal democratic government under President Ebert fled, eventually to Stuttgart.

While the Kappists in Berlin declared a new government, the legal government in flight proclaimed a duty of all citizens to obey only it. The 'Länder' (provinces) were directed to refuse all cooperation with those who had attacked the Republic.

After a strike of workers against the coup broke out in Berlin, Social Democratic leaders of the party and the government called for a general strike. Civil servants and conservative government bureaucrats refused to cooperate with the usurpers. Qualified men rejected posts in the upstart regime. All along the line, people denied authority to the usurpers and refused to assist them. On March 15 the legal government refused to compromise with the usurpers, and the Kappists' power further disintegrated. Leaflets, entitled "The Collapse of the Military Dictatorship," calling for resistance, were showered on the capital by airplane. Some strikers were killed by shooting. On March 17 the Berlin Security Police demanded Kapp's resignation.

The same day, Kapp resigned and fled to Sweden. That night, many of his aides left Berlin in civilian clothes, and General Lüttwitz resigned. Some bloody clashes had occurred in the midst of the predominantly nonviolent noncooperation. The Baltic Brigades then obeyed the legal government and marched out of Berlin, killing and wounding some unsympathetic civilians as they left. The coup was defeated by the combined citizens' action of workers, civil servants, bureaucrats, and the general population. They refused the usurpers the contributions required to make their claims of power effective.

All was still not well. The government then faced attack from another source, as a violent rising by a "Red" army in the Rhineland took many lives. The Weimar Republic, however, had withstood its first frontal attack.[1]

France, 1961: The French case is unusual, in that it began with action of French military officers in Algeria, then ruled by France, in an attempt to block the government intention to give Algeria independence. The French army had for several years been fighting an Algerian guerrilla struggle. For the coup to succeed, a parallel coup would have been needed in France itself, or the rebel French forces in Algeria would have needed to invade France and overthrow the de Gaulle government.

The night of April 21-22, 1961 the French First Foreign Legion Parachute Regiment captured control of Algiers while other military units seized key points nearby. There was no serious opposition. At least three generals in Algeria loyal to the legal government—including the Commander-in-Chief—were arrested. This was the culmination of conflicts between the French army in Algeria and the civilian French government in Paris. President de Gaulle ten days earlier had indicated he was abandoning the attempt to keep Algeria French.

On April 22 the rebel "Military Command" declared a state of siege in Algeria. It announced it was taking over all powers of civil government and would break any resistance. Four colonels had organized the conspiracy, but this statement was issued under the names of four recently retired generals, Challe, Jouhard, Zeller, and Salan. The next day the coup was backed by General Nicot (acting head of the French Air Staff), General Bogot (air force commander in Algiers), and three other generals. The usurpers seized control of newspapers and radio, giving them (they thought) a monopoly of communications in French Algeria.

The French government was in trouble. Half a million French troops were in Algeria, leaving very few operational units in France itself. Two French divisions stationed in Germany were of doubtful reliability. The loyalty of the para-military 'Gendarmerie Nationale' and the 'Compagnies Républicaines de Sécurité' was also in doubt. A parallel coup might be attempted against the government in Paris, or the air force might transport rebel troops to invade France and oust the de Gaulle government.

On Sunday, April 23, the political parties and trade unions in France held mass meetings, calling for a one-hour symbolic general strike the next day to demonstrate they would oppose the coup. That night, de Gaulle broadcast to the French nation, urging defiance and disobedience against the rebels:

> In the name of France, I order that all means—I repeat all means—be employed to bar the way everywhere to these men until they are brought down. I forbid every Frenchman and in the first place, every soldier, to carry out their orders.

The same night, Prime Minister M. Debré in his own broadcast warned of preparations for an airborne attack and closed down the

Paris airport completely. While stressing "all means"—which obviously included military action—Debré placed his confidence in nonmilitary means, as he called for popular action to persuade soldiers who might be landed to resume loyalty to the legal government:

> As soon as the sirens sound, go there [to the airports] by foot or by car, to convince the mistaken soldiers of their huge error.

De Gaulle's broadcast from France was heard in Algeria on transistor radios by the population and members of the military forces, many of them conscript soldiers. Copies of the talk were then duplicated and widely distributed. De Gaulle credited his talk with inducing widespread noncooperation and disobedience against the rebels: "From then on the revolt met with a passive resistance on the spot which became hourly more explicit."

On April 24 at 5 P.M. ten million workers took part in the symbolic general strike. De Galle utilized emergency powers under the constitution. Many right-wing sympathizers were arrested. At airfields vehicles were prepared to be placed on runways to block their use if planes attempted to land. Guards were placed at public buildings. A financial and shipping blockade was imposed on Algeria. That night General Crepin announced that French Forces in Germany were loyal to the government, and the next morning they were ordered to Paris.

French troops in Algeria took loyal action to support the government and undermine the rebels. By Tuesday two-thirds of the available transport planes, and many fighter planes, had been flown out of Algeria, making them unavailable for an invasion of France. Other pilots pretended mechanical failures or blocked airfields. Army soldiers simply stayed in their barracks. There were many cases of deliberate inefficiency: orders from rebel officers got lost; files disappeared; there were delays in communication and transportation. The conscripts generally recognized the power of their noncooperation in support of the legal government. Leaders of the coup had to use many of their available forces to attempt to keep control and order among the French troops in Algeria itself. Many officers sat on the fence, waiting to see how the contest would go.

French civilians in Algeria at first supported the coup, including the Algiers police. But civil servants and local government officials in Algiers often resisted, hiding documents and personally withdrawing so as not to be seen as supporting the coup. On Tuesday evening, the 25th, the Algiers police resumed support for the de Gaulle government. Internal disagreements developed among the leaders of the revolt, with some advocating violent measures. Tuesday night, in another broadcast, de Gaulle ordered loyal troops to fire at the rebels. There was no need, however. The coup had already been fatally undermined.

The leaders resolved to liquidate their own attempted coup. The night of April 25–26, the First Foreign Legion Parachute Regiment withdrew from Algiers, and rebels abandoned government buildings. General Challe surrendered, and the other three retired generals heading the revolt hid.

There were a few casualties, probably three killed and several wounded in Algeria and Paris. The attack had been decisively defeated by defiance and dissolution. De Gaulle remained president, and Algeria became independent in 1962.[2]

IMPROVISED CASES AGAINST INVASIONS

Germany, 1923: Probably the first case in history of nonviolent resistance being official government policy against a foreign invasion was the German struggle in the Ruhr against the French and Belgian occupation in 1923.

The Ruhr struggle is especially complex and covers a period from January 11 to September 26, 1923. It is impossible here to do more than mention some of its features. The invasion aimed to secure scheduled payments of reparations (following the First World War), despite Germany's extreme financial difficulties, and to gain other political objectives (such as separation of the Rhineland from Germany).

The occupation was met with a policy of German noncooperation, which had been decided only days before the actual invasion. There had been no preparations, but the resistance was to be financed by the government. Trade unions had strongly pressured for adoption of the policy. One of their spokesmen had argued that "If civil servants and workers stop work whenever the invaders appear, and the employers refuse to fulfil the demands of the Franco-Belgian commissions, it should be possible to deprive the commissions and military forces of the means for carrying out their tasks."

Actual noncooperation with the invasion forces developed gradually. The means included the refusal to obey the orders of the occupation forces; nonviolent acts of defiance; the refusal of mine owners to serve the invaders; massive demonstrations at courts during trials of resisters; the refusal of German policemen to salute foreign officials; the refusal of German workers to run the railroads for the French; the dismantling of railroad equipment; the refusal of shopkeepers to sell to foreign soldiers; the refusal of people, even when hungry, to use occupier-organized soup kitchens; defiant publication of newspapers in spite of many bans; posting of resistance proclamations and posters; refusal to mine coal; and other methods.

Repression was severe. It included the proclamation of a state of siege; the expulsion of resisters into unoccupied Germany; courts martial; the tolerance of bands of thugs and robbers; trials and long prison sentences; shootings; killings; whippings; the seizure of money and personal property; imprisonment without trial; control of the press; billeting of troops in homes and schools; identity cards; a multitude of regulations; and other means. Widespread food shortages, due to resistance and repressive measures, produced severe hunger.

Resistance was complicated by demolitions which resulted in deaths of occupation personnel. The sabotage was associated with spies and informers, and suspected informers were assassinated. Demolitions also tended to reduce the international shift of sympathy for Germany. The Prussian Minister of the Interior Severing, the trade unions, and the population of the occupied area mostly strongly disapproved of the sabotage by outsiders, which upset the previous unity of the resistance. The sabotage also led to severe reprisals and punishments, both official and spontaneous, by angry occupation soldiers. One such measure was the ban on road traffic. Widespread unemployment and hunger were severe problems, as was continuing extraordinary inflation. The unity and, to a large extent, the will to resist were finally broken.

On 26 September the German government called off the non-cooperation campaign, but the sufferings of the population increased. Complex negotiations occurred. Germany finally stabilized the currency, while facing a series of Communist and extreme right-wing insurrections and attempted coups in various 'Länder'.

Belgians protested widely against their government's actions. Some French people became advocates of the German cause. Toward the end of 1923, Poincaré admitted to the French National Assembly that his policies had failed. Germany could not claim victory, but the invaders finally withdrew. The Rhineland was not detached from

Germany. The invaders had achieved neither their economic nor their political objectives.

Britain and the United States intervened and secured a restructuring of the handling of reparations. The Dawes Plan was developed to deal with reparations, occupation costs, and German financial solvency, and it provided a loan to Germany—all on the basis of the assumption of German unity.

Occupation forces were all withdrawn by June 1925.[3]

Czechoslovakia, 1968–1969: The Czechoslovak case is a most unusual one, and constitutes perhaps the most significant attempt thus far to improvise civilian struggle for national defense purposes. Ultimately, the attempt was defeated, but not quickly. For eight months, the Czechs and Slovaks prevented the Russians from achieving their political objective—a regime responsive to Soviet wishes. It has been reported that the Russians had originally expected military resistance and had estimated they could crush it, install a puppet regime, and then withdraw, all within a few days.

The Soviet leaders thought that invasion by more than a half million Warsaw Treaty Organization troops would crush the Czechoslovak Army and leave the population in confusion and defeat. The invasion would make possible a coup d'état to replace the Dubček reform regime. Accordingly, as soon as possible several of the important Czechoslovak leaders were kidnapped by the K.G.B., including Alexander Dubček, the Communist Party's First Secretary; Prime Minister Oldrich Černik; National Assembly President Josef Smrkovsky; and National Front Chairman Frantisek Kriegel. The President of the Republic, Ludvik Svoboda, was held under house arrest.

There was no Czechoslovak defeat, however, for Czechoslovak officials had given emergency orders for the troops to stay in their barracks. Instead, a very different type of resistance was waged. As a result of the particular character of Czechoslovak resistance, the Soviet officials experienced serious morale problems among the invading troops.

Resistance at several strategic political points prevented establishment of a collaborationist government. Resistance began in the early hours of the invasion as employees of the government news agency refused to issue a press release stating that certain Czechoslovak party and government leaders had requested the invasion. President Svoboda refused to sign a document presented to him by the Stalinist clique. A clandestine radio network called for peaceful resistance, reported on resistance activities, and convened several official bodies which opposed the invasion.

Government and party leaders and bodies denounced the invasion. The National Assembly demanded release of the arrested leaders, and the immediate withdrawal of the foreign troops. Broadcasters on the clandestine radio network during the first week helped to create many forms of resistance and shape others. The same means were used to convene the Extraordinary Fourteenth Party Congress, call one-hour general strikes, request rail workers to slow the transport of Russian tracking and jamming equipment, and discourage collaboration. These broadcasts were also to argue the futility of violent resistance and the wisdom of nonviolent struggle. It was impossible for the Russians to find sufficient collaborators to set up their puppet regime.

Militarily totally successful, the Russians found they could not control the country. In the face of unified civilian resistance and the increasing demoralization of their troops, the Soviet leaders flew President Svoboda to Moscow for negotiations, but once there, Svoboda insisted on the presence of the arrested Czechoslovak leaders.

A compromise—which was probably a major strategic mistake—was worked out which legitimized the presence of Soviet troops and sacrificed some of the Czechoslovak reforms. Many of the basic reforms were maintained, however, and the country's leaders were returned to Prague to their official positions. The general population saw the compromise as a defeat, however, and for a week would not accept it.

Despite weaknesses and compromises, the reform regime and many of its liberalization measures were maintained from August until the following April, when some anti-Russian rioting provided the pretext for intensified Russian pressure. This time the Czechoslovak leadership capitulated, ousting the Dubček reform group from their party and government positions, and replacing them with the hard-line Husak regime.

The Russians had been forced to shift from their initial military means to gradual political pressures and manipulations, and had experienced an eight-month delay in gaining their basic objective. Against such overwhelming odds, if Czechoslovak military resistance had held off full Russian control for that long, the struggle would have been classed with the Battle of Thermopylae.

The nature and accomplishments of the Czechoslovak defense are already forgotten by many, and when remembered, they are usually distorted. The resistance ultimately failed, but it prevented full Soviet control from August 1968 until April 1969. That would have been impossible with military means. The resistance also reportedly caused such severe morale problems among Russian troops that all troops in the original invasion force had to be rotated out of the country in a few days and sent, not to European Russia where they could report what was happening, but to Siberia.

All this was done without preparation and training, much less contingency planning. This experience suggests, even in final defeat (as a result of capitulation by Czechoslovak officials, not defeated resistance), that this technique possesses a power potential even greater than military means.[4]

These and other improvised cases merit careful research, study, and analysis. Not all such experiments have succeeded. (Nor have all prepared military defense struggles succeeded.) These prototypes demonstrate—simply because they have occurred—that nonviolent struggle for defense is possible and can be powerful.

A POLICY TO DETER AND DEFEND

Civilian-based defense is an alternative defense policy which builds upon this improvised past experience, adding to it deliberate refinement through research, policy studies, feasibility studies, contingency planning, preparations, and training. This policy is designed to deter and defeat not only foreign military invasions and occupations but also internal take-overs. This policy may be applied (1) as a supplement to military means, (2) in place of them in special circumstances only (as against a coup d'état or when the military forces have been defeated), or (3) as a permanent and complete substitute defense policy.

Deterrence and defense are to be accomplished by civilian forms of struggle—social, economic, political, and psychological. Many kinds of political noncooperation, strikes, economic boycotts, symbolic protests, civil disobedience, social boycotts, and more extreme methods of disruption and intervention are among the weapons of this policy. These are used to wage widespread noncooperation and to offer massive public defiance. The aims are to deny the attackers their objectives and to make their society politically indigestible and ungovernable by attackers. Consolidation of foreign rule, a puppet government, or a government of usurpers becomes impossible. In addition, the civilian defenders aim to subvert the loyalty of the aggressors' troops and functionaries, to make them unreliable in carrying out orders and repression, and even to induce them to mutiny.

Deterrence against invasions and internal usurpations is achieved by a strong capacity to defend. Potential attackers are deterred when they see that their objectives will be denied them, political consolidation prevented, and that as a consequence of these struggles unacceptable costs will be imposed on them politically, economically, and internationally.

The term "civilian-based defense" thus indicates defense by civilians using civilian means of struggle. This policy has also been called "civilian defense," "social defense," "nonmilitary defense," "nonviolent defense," "popular nonviolent defense," and "defense by civil resistance."

Civilian-based defense measures are applied by the general population, particular groups, and the society's institutions. The groups and institutions most involved will be those most affected by the attackers' objectives—economic, ideological, political, or other—and therefore best situated to resist them.

In this type of conflict the defenders deliberately seek to fight by using a technique of struggle with which military aggressors cannot easily deal. This is an asymmetrical conflict situation, one in which the two sides are fighting by contrasting means of combat. Since it is foolish to choose to fight with your enemy's best weapons, to have a chance at success the defenders must stick to their own chosen nonviolent weapons system. (This is discussed again briefly in Chapter 6.)

Viable deterrence and defense by this civilian-based policy are possible because violence is not the source of power in politics. The source is, instead, the cooperation of people and human institutions—which can be refused. Auguste Comte argued in the early nineteenth century that the then popular theory that attributed to rulers a permanent, unchanging degree of power was not correct. On the contrary, he insisted, the power of a ruler is variable and depends on the degree to which the society grants him that power.[5] Baron de Montesquieu observed that "those who govern have a power which, in some measure, has need of fresh vigor every day. . . . "[6] Even sanctions—punishments—as a source of power depend on the society.

Not only does the capacity to impose sanctions rest on cooperation; the effectiveness of threatened or applied sanctions depends on the response of the subjects against whom they are directed.

Civilian-based defense, and nonviolent struggle generally, can wield great power, even against ruthless rulers and military regimes, because they attack the most vulnerable characteristic of all hierarchical institutions and governments: dependence on the submission and cooperation of the governed.

The rulers of governments and political systems are not omnipotent, nor do they possess self-generating power. All rulers depend for the sources of their power—authority, economic resources, skills and knowledge, intangible factors (such as attitudes to obedience), administration, and even sanctions—upon the cooperation of the population and the institutions of the society they would rule. The availability of those sources depends on the cooperation and obedience of many groups and institutions, special personnel, and the general population. The restriction or withdrawal of cooperation and obedience will directly and indirectly reduce or sever the availability of those sources of power.

If noncooperation and disobedience against an unwanted ruler can be applied and maintained—usually in face of repression intended to force resumption of cooperation and obedience—then the capacity of that regime to rule and to maintain its position is threatened. If, despite that repression, the sources of power can be restricted, withheld, or severed for sufficient time, the result may be the political paralysis of the regime. In severe cases the ruler's power will progressively die—slowly or rapidly—from political starvation.[7] This is what occurred in Imperial Russia in February 1917, El Salvador and Guatemala in 1944, Iran in 1979, and the Philippines in 1986.

This insight into the nature and vulnerability of political power and the widespread experience in nonviolent struggle listed in Table One establish that we are dealing with a type of struggle which is not restricted by cultural or national boundaries.[8] Civilian-based defense is, therefore, potentially relevant to problems of international aggression and internal usurpation in all parts of the world.

The many improvised cases of nonviolent struggle against oppression and aggression can be viewed as applications of this fundamental insight into the nature of power. Unfortunately, sophisticated rulers and aggressors have often been more aware of their dependence on the people and society than their subjects and victims of aggression

Table One.   Improvised Cases of Civilian Struggle.[9]

Cases of Nonviolent Insurrections and Revolutions
Against Domestic Dictatorial Rule

Russian Revolution of 1905

Persian Revolution of 1905–1906

Russian Revolution of February 1917

Economic shut-down and political noncooperation in El Salvador against the Hernández Martínez regime, 1944

Economic shut-down and political noncooperation in Guatemala against the Ubico regime, 1944

East German uprising, June 1953

General strike and economic shut-down against Haitian strongman General Magliore, 1956

Hungarian Revolution, 1956–1957

South Vietnamese Buddhist undermining of the Ngo Dinh Diem regime, 1963

Sudanese civilian insurrection against General Abboud's regime, 1964

Thai civilian uprising of October 1973

Iranian revolution against the Shah, 1978–1979

Polish democratization movement by Solidarity, 1980– ?

Haitian civil rising against "Baby Doc" Duvalier, 1986

Philippine nonviolent insurrection against President Marcos, 1986

Cases of National Resistance to Established Foreign Domination

---

Major aspects of the Netherlands' resistance to Spanish rule, 1565–1576

American colonial noncooperation campaigns against British laws, taxes, and rule, 1765–1775

Hungarian nonviolent resistance to Austrian rule, 1850–1867

Finnish resistance to Russian rule, 1898–1905

Egyptian nonviolent protests and noncooperation to British rule, 1919–1922

Korean national protest against Japanese rule, 1919–1922

Western Samoan resistance to New Zealand rule, 1919–1936

Indian independence struggles, especially the campaigns of 1930–1931, 1932–1934, 1940–1941, and 1942

Cases of Noncooperation Against Coups d'État and Other
Internal Usurpations

German general strike and political noncooperation against the Kapp 'Putsch,' 1920

Table One. continued

General strike in Haiti against temporary President Pierre-Louis, 1957

French popular resistance, government calls for defiance, and soldiers' noncooperation against the Algiers generals' 'Putsch,' 1961

Noncooperation to defeat a military coup d'état in Bolivia, 1978

Polish noncooperation against the regime of General Jaruzelski, 1981- ?

Cases of Resistance Against Recent Foreign Invasions,
Occupations, and Puppet Governments

German government-sponsored nonviolent resistance in the Ruhr against the French and Belgian occupation, 1923

Major aspects of the Dutch resistance, including several important strikes, against the German occupation, 1940–1945

Major aspects of the Danish resistance, including the 1944 Copenhagen general strike, against the German occupation, 1940–1945

Major aspects of the Norwegian resistance to the Quisling regime and German occupation, 1940–1945

Noncooperation and defiance to save Jews in Nazi-occupied countries, 1940–1945, especially in Bulgaria, Denmark, Norway, the Netherlands, Belgium, France, and Italy

Czechoslovak resistance to the Soviet and Warsaw Pact invasion and occupation, 1968–1969

---

have been. People have often thought they were helpless before threatening and brutal rulers whose power was in reality vulerable and fragile.

RESOURCES FOR DEVELOPING
CIVILIAN-BASED DEFENSE

Civilian-based defense becomes possible when people come to understand the power which they and their institutions can wield against potential aggressors, and prepare themselves to apply that power effectively. Civilian-based defense is not simply improvised or spontaneous resistance, as almost all past cases of nonviolent struggle have been. Instead, this policy is to be waged on the basis of advance preparations, planning, and training. Prior research and policy studies will help in planning the defense. This will increase its effectiveness in paralyzing the attackers' policies and in defeating their repression, especially against ruthless regimes. Strategies of civilian-based defense are more likely to be successful if they are based on an understanding both of the requirements for effective nonviolent struggle and also of the ways to aggravate the weaknesses of the attackers' system. This includes its political, social, and economic aspects as well as its occupation administration or system of governance.

In short, civilian-based defense aims to deter and defeat attacks by making a society ungovernable by would-be oppressors and by maintaining a capacity for orderly self-rule even in face of extreme threats and actual aggression. To the degree that people find this policy to be effective for defense, and thereby for deterrence, it becomes possible for societies to reduce reliance on, and eventually to phase out, military means. Proponents of this policy call for thorough investigation and rigorous examination of its potential.

While civilian-based defense is nonviolent, it is not pacifism. This policy can be applied effectively by persons who have supported or used violence in the past and might again in the future under other circumstances. This defense policy simply requires that they adhere to nonviolent means of struggle as part of a grand strategy for the course of the given conflict. Some pacifists would back civilian-based defense, while others would not. Overwhelmingly, the major nonviolent struggle campaigns of the past have been waged by masses of people who were never pacifists. Whole societies could therefore shift from military to civilian means of defense without deep changes in millions of individuals. Such a transition might well be made with fewer difficulties and in less time than most people have thought.

At first glance, civilian-based defense may appear to some people to be an unreasonable proposal. It may be thought that national security would be jeopardized by giving up a military-based defense system for an alternative security system that is untried and untested. This view, however, overlooks the fact that many military weapons are themselves unprecedented and untested in combat. On the other hand, nonviolent struggle—the basis of civilian-based defense—has a long history. Its consequences, therefore, may not only be less destructive than those of the new military weapons systems, but may also be much more calculable.

For many decades, military preparations have been characterized not only by refinement of older types of weaponry but also by development of new ones, even whole new types which never previously existed. In recent decades vast economic and intellectual resources have been devoted to developing and procuring weapons that were unprecedented. Rather than a disadvantage, their novelty has been usually seen as a positive quality. Governments have been not only willing but eager to apply them in war, as in the German use of rockets against England during the Second World War, the American use of atomic bombs against Japan in 1945, and the use of several new weapons during the Falklands War of 1982.

Civilian-based defense is not so extreme a projection beyond experience as was the proposal in 1939 to President Roosevelt to explore development of a whole new type of explosive from nuclear fission. In the case of civilian-based defense, there have been—as cited in this and the previous chapter—a number of improvised experiments with nonviolent struggle against domestic and foreign domination and for national defense objectives.

All new military weapons and all policies and strategies based on innovative weapons (including those of NATO) lack historical verification of their ability to fulfil the intended objectives. The scenarios for NATO defense of Western Europe against a possible Soviet sweep westward by use of theater nuclear weapons in Europe are mostly based on untested assumptions, conjectures, and guesses, and not on carefully examined experience. The only experience with the wartime use of atomic weapons—at Hiroshima and Nagasaki—is mostly ignored and excluded from European strategic calculations. The human consequences of the atomic bombings of Japan suggest that plans for the use of nuclear weapons in Europe to defend the peoples of Western Europe are not based on serious calculations of their likely results. Supporters of present NATO policies are, therefore, in no position to dismiss civilian-based defense categorically on the basis that there is no historical experience of its planned application by a fully trained population.

As a prepared policy to be waged by a trained population, civilian-based defense is only now being developed. It is a projection from past improvised experience to a possible future prepared defense policy. Civilian-based defense is rooted in the general technique of "nonviolent action" as it has been widely used in improvised forms in the past.[10] Nonviolent action might also be called "civilian struggle." This technique has been far more important in history than has previously been recognized. Some of the more significant cases, arranged in four groups, are listed in Table One. Note that this type of conflict has been used not only in resistance and revolution against oppression but also in several national defense struggles.

This type of combat has almost always been launched without advance decision, planning, preparations, and training. Except for limited previous experience and restricted improvisation based on largely unknown cases elsewhere, both the leaders and participants in nonviolent struggles have always had to act without the most basic resources available to military practitioners for thousands of years. These include thorough knowledge of the technique being used, strategic principles, prior organization, weapons development, and instruction in the needed skills. There have naturally been defeats: the Korean national resistance to the Japanese in 1919–1922, for example. In other cases the results have been mixed, as in the 1923 German struggle in the Ruhr. Outright victories have also been won, such as the ousting of the military dictator of El Salvador in 1944 and the defeat of Quisling's plans for the Corporate State in Norway during the Nazi occupation.

Just as for many centuries deliberate efforts have increased the combat capacity of military conflict, so research, strategic analysis, preparation, and training should multiply our capacity to gain objectives by nonviolent struggle generally, and specifically to provide deterrence and defense by civilian-based sanctions.

CONSIDERING THE NEW POLICY

Can civilian-based defense be developed to meet the defense and security needs of Western European countries more adequately and with fewer grave problems than present policies? The answer to this question is likely to shape much of the future of Europe and to influence the international system in the decades ahead.

In recent years the civilian-based defense option has been receiving increasing attention from the general public in Western European countries. In some cases, the policy has begun to receive limited consideration by governments, for example in Sweden and the Netherlands. The degree to which this policy is explored and adopted will largely be determined by the estimate made of its effectiveness in comparison to other options. It seems probable that civilian-based defense can meet the deterrence and defense needs of Western European countries more adequately than present policies, while reducing significantly the dangers of destruction of their societies and the annihilation of their peoples. If so, civilian-based defense, by its capacity to deter or defeat a possible Soviet invasion, could provide an alternative to nuclear war.

In several countries scholars and others have begun to investigate the utility of nonmilitary forms of struggle as a possible supplement to military means or as a full alternative to provide deterrence and defense against aggression.[11] However, this work, while impressive, remains rudimentary in comparison to the results of centuries of study devoted to conventional military strategy and tactics. In this infant stage of development, civilian-based defense certainly has problems which require careful consideration. These problems will need to be compared to those of present policies. No perfect policy exists. No policy, military or civilian, is free of risks and costs, nor can the consequences of any policy be guaranteed.

Nevertheless, the risks and costs inherent in today's military and civilian-based security policies for Western Europe are not equal. The capacities and possible consequences of each policy can be evaluated and compared, with a reasonable degree of validity. Detailed evaluation of civilian-based defense will require research, analysis, feasibility studies, preparations, training, and finally, as with all policies, application in a crisis. It is possible, however, to begin here to explore the relevance of the civilian-based defense policy for Western Europe.

The policy must meet the needs of particular countries of Western Europe; their diversity must be recognized. When we speak of "Europe" and "Europeans" we lose a great deal of precision. The European nations have a common civilization and their political systems are often very similar. However, each country differs in culture and geography, and usually in language and climate. They also vary significantly in social, economic, and political conditions. They also differ in specific defense and security needs, including the degree to which the threats to national security come from internal groups or from foreign states.

The neutral and nonaligned countries—Finland, Austria, Ireland, Switzerland, Sweden, and Yugoslavia—are so different from one another that they can only be grouped together for consideration of the most general problems and needs. Individual studies are required for each of these countries on its possible receptivity to civilian-based defense and on the capacity of the policy to meet perceived security needs. Each of the minor NATO partners—Norway, Denmark, Iceland, the Netherlands, Spain, Portugal, Belgium, Luxembourg, Greece, and Turkey—and each of the major European members—West Germany, Britain, Italy, and France (in its special relationship)—require individual consideration. The situations of the North American members—Canada and the United States—are still different.

In all these societies the motives for adopting and applying civilian-based defense would be the same as have long been the case with military means: love of one's own country; belief in the right of a people to choose its own political system and government; opposition to international aggression, internal usurpations, and foreign domination; belief in a religious or moral duty to protect one's homeland and people; conviction that however imperfect one's own society, its defense against foreign aggressors and internal usurpers is a prerequisite to building a better one; and agreement that, however much people may disagree among themselves, no outside state or internal clique will be allowed to dominate them.

Both "minimalist" and "maximalist" positions may be relevant in considering what role civilian-based defense measures might have in the defense policy of any given country. Let us look first at the policy from a minimalist perspective.

A country might add a modest civilian-based defense component to its defense policy alongside its military posture with the aims of: (1) increasing the deterrent effect of its overall policy by making visible preparations to continue defense even after occupation; (2) deterring and defeating internal or foreign-instigated coups d'état or other usurpations; (3) mollifying a strong peace movement or anti-nuclear weapons movement; (4) emphasizing the strictly defensive intent of the overall policy; (5) meeting the demand of a smaller political party needed for a coalition government; or (6) reducing the dangers of escalation to nuclear war by providing an active defense alternative when conventional military means appear or have proven to be inadequate.

Not only nuclear destruction but also surrender could be avoided by simply adding to present policies one additional "layer" (or more) of unorthodox means of defense. In extreme crises that country or alliance could then shift its strategy from nuclear options to these unconventional means. Civilian-based defense might be used after a conventional military defeat to avoid surrender. (That has the disadvantage, of course, of the country having already experienced many casualties and massive destruction.) The civilian component might also replace the military one earlier, at a point of great danger—as when it is clear that further reliance on military means might escalate to nuclear war. In each case the aim would then be to deny invaders their objectives and to prevent their establishing effective political control, much as in regular civilian-based defense struggle. Those cases would lack, however, some of the psychological advantages accruing to a country which had not been a military enemy or threat.

Questions often arise about permanently combining civilian-based defense with one or both of the other basic defensive postures: defensive conventional military means and guerrilla warfare. Answers to these depend to a large degree on understanding the capabilities, requirements, means of operation (or mechanisms) of both civilian-based defense and military (or para-military) struggle.

Most countries are likely to begin by simply adding a civilian-based defense component to their predominantly military posture, as has already begun to happen. Later, in a series of limited steps, they could expand the role of the nonmilitary option until full reliance on civilian-based defense became a serious prospect. Consideration of civilian-based defense as a full substitute policy would require comparing it with other possible policies for providing defense and security for Western European countries.

Even if the intent is to shift completely to civilian-based defense, it is projected that the process of change-over—called "transarmament"—from the previous military system would require a considerable period of time, as discussed in Chapter 3. During this period the civilian-based capacity would be built up, while the military capacity for some time remained in place.

The maximalist position is a more ambitious goal: the eventual development of civilian-based defense into a full alternative security policy. It would aim to provide self-reliance in deterrence and defense, significantly reduce nuclear dangers, and enhance both security and political freedom.

Why would a society that has long relied upon military means transarm fully to civilian-based defense? The following factors are likely to be included in such a consideration: (1) recognition of the limitations of military means in light of the military superiority of possible attackers; (2) expectation of greater chances of success by this alternative policy against specific threats; (3) desire for increased self-reliance in defense and foreign policies; (4) calculations of significantly less destruction and loss of life in the defending country; (5) perceptions of major economic advantages derived from far lower economic costs of the new policy, and from the shifting of production away from nonproductive weapons to products which increase capital resources or meet social needs; (6) calculations that civilian-based defense will directly and indirectly enhance the future general security of the country; (7) determination that the effects of the policy on the nature of the society itself are more beneficial than those of the military options; and (8) acceptance of the view that civilian-based defense provides a way out of the spiralling development of military technology and the nuclear arms race and toward a reduction and discarding of weapons of mass destruction. Careful attention is required to each of these factors in a possible shift to civilian-based defense.

Recognition of the practical advantages of the new policy is essential to serious consideration of it as an alternative to military policies. Once civilian-based defense is accepted as having practical advantages in preventing and defending against attacks, its nonviolent nature is likely to inspire endorsements of it as ethically, morally, or religiously superior to options which inflict destruction and death. Endorsements of the new policy as only being ethically superior to military means, prior to recognition of civilian-based defense as practically superior, are unlikely to lead to acceptance of the new policy.

The consideration and adoption of civilian-based defense are facilitated by the fact that it does not require people to accept a new political doctrine, party program, or religion, much less a belief in "nonviolence" as a moral or religious principle.[12] People can retain their chosen outlooks and beliefs, and their views about the necessity or rightness of past wars, and still accept the new policy as the wisest and most effective for the present situation. Over time, they might (or might not) modify or change their world-views. However, such a change is in no way a precondition for accepting the viability of the new policy. Persons and groups which, to the contrary, claim that a particular doctrine or "ism" is tied to civilian-based defense should be treated with caution. They may be primarily interested in promoting their beliefs rather than in developing a new defense option to be evaluated dispassionately by people of diverse convictions.

This policy does require, of course, that people be genuinely concerned with the defense and security of their society rather than with other goals for which military means have been used. Examples of the latter are providing an attack capacity, defending an empire, or attaining "great power status"—a term which sounds superior to the actual condition.

In summary, if we examine the potential power of nonviolent struggle against foreign occupations and coups in light of the inadequacies of present policies and of the great military capacities available to the Soviet Union, we find strong reasons for Western European countries to explore seriously this option. As a minimum step, these countries could well improve their security position by moving to add a civilian-based component to their existing defense and deterrence policies, and if they already have such a nonviolent resistance component they might gain by making it more explicit and more adequately prepared.

3 TRANSARMAMENT

THE PROCESS OF TRANSARMAMENT

Transarmament is the process of changing over from a military system to a civilian-based defense system. The transarmament process would in most cases occur over a period of some years. During this time the civilian-based defense capacity would be introduced as a component of the total defense policy, then gradually built up and expanded. At appropriate stages the military components would be phased down and replaced. In some cases a society might not transarm fully but instead retain both military and civilian-based components in some combination. Transarmament always involves the replacement of one means to provide defense and deterrence with another and not, as with disarmament, simply the reduction or abandonment of military capacity.[1]

Civilian-based defense differs from the past cases of nonviolent struggle for national defense in that it is a deliberately chosen and prepared policy, no longer improvised in the midst of crises. Improvisation is likely to continue, of course, in other countries which have not had the opportunity or foresight to prepare. Indeed, as general knowledge of nonviolent struggle spreads, more societies are likely to improvise civilian resistance against foreign invasions and internal usurpations, as Czechoslovakia did in 1968.

It is not a long jump from past cases and continuing improvisation to preparations and training for deterrence and defence against future attacks, but it is a necessary one. While spontaneity often has its positive qualities, it also has serious weaknesses. In crises when quick decisions are often required, it is usually easier to repeat familiar responses to past situations—even when those actions have failed—than to innovate a brilliant strategic move. Improvised struggles often lack forethought and needed groundwork. It is better to make defense shifts when time is available for evaluation, decision, planning, preparations, and training. These will increase the new policy's effectiveness.

The needed research, policy studies, development, and evaluation of means of preparation and training can be initially conducted by private institutions, governmental and military bodies in individual countries, groups of countries or treaty partners (such as NATO), regional organizations, or United Nations agencies.

Because of the nature of nonviolent struggle, it is feasible in civilian-based defense to avoid at least much of the secrecy associated with military methods.[2] (The role of secrecy in specific preparations and during defense struggles, as in leadership and means of communication, in a separate topic.) This makes possible widespread sharing of general knowledge and information among countries investigating the policy and those which have introduced it. Research results, policy analyses, plans and experience in preparations and training, and insights into the nature and goals of potential attackers can be shared with benefit. So, too, can studies of strategy, responses to particular types of attack, means to increase effectiveness, methods of maintaining resistance in face of repression, and ways to meet the society's basic needs in crises.

International cooperation and assistance can therefore be helpful both in the early period of initial investigation and consideration and also in the later period of preparations and training. If, during this time, potential attackers learn more about the capacity of civilian-based defense and preparations for it, that is to the good. That increased knowledge contributes to the deterrent effect of this policy.

Consideration of civilian-based defense and the transarmament process requires a series of steps operating over a period of time. These include: (1) a major program of public education and discussion about the policy, its nature, risks, costs, and potential benefits; (2) research and policy studies into the capabilities, problems, and potential of civilian-based defense, initiated by independent groups, universities, research institutions, governments, and military bodies; (3) evaluation of the policy by the appropriate governmental bodies and other institutions, followed by decisions on whether to introduce it alongside the military capacity; (4) progressive introduction of the new policy as part of the overall, still predominantly military, policy; (5) gradual expansion of the civilian-based defense component; and (6) at a later stage, consideration of whether to keep both the civilian and the military components indefinitely (and, if so, in what proportions), or whether to rely fully on civilian-based defense and to phase out the military sector as no longer needed and potentially counterproductive. The first three of these steps—education, research, and evaluation—can proceed side by side, while the others concerned with policy adoption are likely to follow in sequence.

The time required to initiate the first steps in the transarmament process and to carry it to completion will vary widely with the country and situation. Some countries face grave security threats of invasion, and their military capacities are highly limited. Yet they cannot, or will not, join an alliance. Austria is an example. Such countries might relatively quickly adopt civilian-based defense, partially or fully, to increase their defense capacities. (A similar situation could exist in face of dangers of internal coups d'état.) In such cases, even an inadequately developed civilian-based defense policy would likely be superior to a military option and therefore accepted by policy makers and the general population. Adoption, in full or in part, therefore could happen before major research and other studies have been completed. After further research and more adequate preparations, the capacity of that civilian policy is likely to increase significantly.

Except for such special cases, however, rapid shifts to civilian-based defense are not to be expected and may even be undesirable. That is because poorly planned and implemented civilian-based defense—adopted without careful consideration or fundamental understanding and lacking in adequate strategic planning, preparations, and training—may produce defense disasters. Those may then lead to later abandonment of the policy in that country and to the discrediting of it elsewhere.

In most cases, evaluation of the policy and transarmament to it will (and should) be a gradual and phased process, operating over some years. This time is initially required to provide enhanced understanding of the policy and its potential. Time is also required to produce feasibility studies and contingency plans for meeting various types of attack, to make possible an extended public consideration of the policy, to plan well for the adoption and implementation of the policy, to achieve effective training of the population, and to prepare the society's institutions for their defense roles. Those stages are all highly important and in most situations can be bypassed or abbreviated only with very serious risks. The extended process of transarmament also makes it possible for the overwhelming bulk of the society to embrace the new policy as a paradigm shift. That is preferable to adoption as the result of the defeat of the policy's opponents following a bitter divisive conflict throughout the society. The latter path might produce unfortunate results for both the country and the policy.

Since the general citizenry and the society's institutions are themselves combatants in civilian-based defense struggles, large-scale comprehensive training and preparations would be necessary for the whole population. This would include specialized programs for members of the society's various institutions, occupations, and communities. Training would aim to maximize effective use by the population of social, economic, psychological, and political power against an invader or internal usurper, and to increase people's ability to continue resistance despite repression.[3]

Preparations would also include measures to meet political and economic needs under emergency conditions created by the attack and the defense struggle. Those preparations would include a variety of measures, such as plans and equipment for communicating among the defenders and with the outside world and ways of dealing with severance of usual supplies of food, water, and fuel.[4] Identification is required not only of needs likely to occur in most situations but also of those which may be specific to particular countries and circumstances. Determination of how to meet those needs is also required. Economic conversion from military to civilian production would also be a highly important part of the planned adjustments during the latter years of the transarmament period.[5]

Transarmament to civilian-based defense does not require the prior transformation of the international system, the disappearance of military threats, or universal adoption of the policy. Instead, civilian-based defense is designed to operate in highly imperfect political and international situations and to deter and defend against attacks. Assuming effectiveness of the policy, therefore, civilian-based defense can be adopted by single countries, groups of countries, or alliances, without any wider agreement in the international community, just as new military weapons systems have been.

During the transarmament process the initial civilian-based defense component can be expanded in stages. It is not, however, necessary to decide at the beginning of the process how far that expansion should go. Indeed, the new knowledge derived from the ongoing research and the experience from the preparations, training, and new improvised applications elsewhere will be useful in making decisions at later points on whether to expand the role of civilian-based defense.

The fact that initial steps in exploring and preparing civilian-based defense can be taken while leaving to a future time decisions on how far to proceed greatly facilitates the policy's early development. This makes it possible, for example, for both those who support and those who are critical of present national or NATO military preparations to unite in supporting development of a civilian-based defense component. Supporters of military measures can view the new component as simply an extra layer of deterrence and defense added to present policies, thereby increasing their depth and flexibility. Critics of present policies may, on the other hand, reasonably hope that—as more is learned about the power capacity of civilian-based defense—the supporters of present military policies will join in supporting progressive expansion of the new component. Expanding civilian-based defense to replace military means fully is not in any sense inevitable, however. Some countries might keep both capacities for long periods of time.

The general model presented by theorists of civilian-based defense, however, is for a full transarmament, in stages and over some years, instead of a permanent combination of military and civilian means. Even in the process of full transarmament, however, the military capability would not be downgraded or eliminated until the society and government perceived sufficient reason to be confident in the capacity of civilian-based defense to deter and defend against attacks, with clear advantages over a military posture.

Civilian-based defense policy allows considerable flexibility to countries adopting it in the scope and framework of their security arrangements and the content of their foreign policies. Let us look at the security arrangements here, and then, in the next section, at alternative international political stances for a transarmed country.

As one option, a country transarming to civilian-based defense could choose a very independent security policy. Such a country would avoid all defense agreements and alliances, choosing instead to rely on its own resources and to avoid the complications alliances might bring. Today, in a military context, for example, Switzerland, while active internationally in certain ways, has no military alliances and even has refused to join the United Nations. A self-reliant civilian-based security policy, however, does not exclude an active foreign policy and participation in international organizations.

Instead of opting for a wholly self-reliant security policy, a civilian-based defense country could choose to cooperate with other countries in its security policy. While most countries are likely to explore and adopt civilian-based defense one at a time, some may do so as part of a decision by an existing military or political alliance or as a consequence of a negotiated multi-state agreement. Those countries are likely to assist one another during the transarmament period in the ways discussed above. During actual crises, with one country under attack and the others not, assistance could be provided to the defending society on the plane of overt popular resistance by such means as assisting communications, providing food, and by applying economic and political sanctions against the invader. Any appearance of foreign direction of the society's defense struggle should be avoided.

Both types of international assistance and cooperation might operate informally. They might also be developed on the basis of limited agreements and understandings or formal treaties. These mutual assistance arrangements might be organized on a regional basis. The Nordic countries—Sweden, Norway, Finland, Denmark, and Iceland—are a possible such grouping. They share similar heritages and cultures, closely related languages to a large degree, and similar climatic conditions and geopolitical situations; they already cooperate formally and informally in various ways. Indeed, despite very significant present differences in their international situations and foreign and security policies, some or all members of the Nordic Council might add civilian-based defense components to their present security policies in parallel actions or even jointly planned developments.

Wider cooperative arrangements are also possible. In 1958 British Commander Sir Stephen King-Hall suggested that the European countries which had transarmed and abandoned nuclear weapons might form a European Treaty Organization for mutual nonmilitary defense assistance.[6] NATO itself could, by alliance decision, request that its members add a civilian-based defense component to their present policies and provide support and assistance for that introduction and for its continuing development and potential expansion.

Some of the ways such an alliance would help in applying civilian-based defense are outlined in Chapter 6 of this book. As compared with foreign military aid in the midst of a war, the nonviolent character of the defense resistance and the international aid is likely to reduce (though not eliminate) the chance that the assisting country may become actively involved in the conflict. Depending on the situation, certain kinds of international support could prove to be extremely helpful to the civilian defenders and contribute to their ability to defeat the attack.

ALTERNATIVE POLITICAL STANCES

Whether a transarming country chooses an independent or a cooperative version of civilian-based defense, it could pursue any one of a number of quite different, and even contrasting, international political stances. Three of these are discussed briefly here. More are possible, even economically selfish and largely inward-looking ones.

First, a transarmed country might choose to operate politically on the international scene in a purely defensive way. It would simply seek to live in accordance with its chosen system and way of life, changing or maintaining them as it wished. It would not seek to pronounce on or to influence the internal systems of other countries. It would allow other countries to deal with their own political problems without becoming involved and without seeking to influence the outcomes, beyond the influence of transactions normally occurring in today's interdependent world. Some countries might even seek to reduce their international ties and to become more self-reliant economically as well as politically. Taking this defensive posture would not, however, prevent a country from actively engaging in humanitarian assistance, medical aid, famine and disaster relief, and the like. Present Swiss policies are the closest approximation to this posture. Other countries might not be so altruistic.

Second, countries could combine civilian-based defense with a highly participatory internationalist political stance. The transarmed country might, for example, aim to contribute positively to improved international understanding. Hence, programs encouraging those aims could be undertaken or expanded. They could include: educational activities; student exchanges; cultural tours; tourist visits; "twinning" of cities; learning programs on languages, society, culture, and history; and increased direct personal contacts.

At the same time, the civilian-based defense country with this internationalist political policy could participate actively in bilateral and multilateral programs of economic aid and development of self-sufficiency in food and livelihood for poorer countries and hungry populations. Other international programs might focus on the fields of health, nutrition, energy, education, science, and others. In some cases, international support and cooperation might be launched to help resolve some particularly serious problem in one or more countries, such as Apartheid in South Africa. One aim of these internationalist activities might be to reduce serious conflicts which might contribute to future wars.

Third, a country relying on civilian-based defense could combine that policy with an offensive international political stance, aiming to spread its own political outlook and system and to undermine antithetical ones. As a public policy civilian-based defense is naturally defensive. It can, however, be combined with a political position which is actively hostile to particular conditions and regimes and seeks to change or undermine them, especially dictatorial, undemocratic, racist, or oppressive ones. This may involve using nonviolent international political and economic sanctions and spreading knowledge of how to wage nonviolent struggle to the population of the countries with those conditions and disliked regimes. This is facilitated by the fact that nonviolent action tends to be democratizing; hence, it contributes to the undermining of oppressive élite domination.[7]

Civilian-based defense countries might take an offensive political stance against regimes that were extreme dictatorships, or those that seriously maltreated part of their own population or imposed a system of social oppression. Other targets could be regimes that were killing large numbers of people, preparing for genocide, preparing to attack other countries militarily, actively promoting a noxious ideology, or actively assisting terrorist groups.

The transarmed countries taking an offensive position might act against such a regime in various ways. These include: making radio broadcasts to its population of suppressed news and of views attacking the regime and supporting opposition; imposing diplomatic and economic sanctions; actively promoting news and views inimical to the foreign regime; translating and disseminating information on how to disintegrate dictatorships and how to wage nonviolent struggle effectively against oppressive systems; and perhaps even providing financial and other assistance to opposition groups, both within and outside the country itself.

These offensive political activities would be intended to help modify or disintegrate the opposed regime to benefit its own oppressed population or to prevent military aggression against the civilian-based defense country, or both.

Even for these aims and using only nonviolent means, such foreign intervention can create problems and pose serious dangers of external interference and domination. This can occur as a result of applying patterns of action which could later be used without discretion for very different objectives, or which despite good motives contribute to disaster. For example, dictatorial countries might apply nonviolent sanctions against democratic societies and promote internal agitation and financial disruption to help destroy their system. Serious dangers can occur when the external group takes on the responsibility of initiating fundamental changes which belong primarily to the people of that society. To reduce such dangers, the offensive activities discussed above should at most support domestic opposition to the disliked regime. It is important that its home population become able to replace the old oppressive ruling group with a significantly better system. The destruction of the disliked regime should not be accomplished primarily by foreign action and manipulation. Even if temporarily successful, the results would not be likely to last; the oppressed population would probably remain as weak as ever and could easily fall prey to another dominating élite, possibly one worse than the ousted one.

Whichever political stance a civilian-based defense country might take—defensive, internationalist, or offensive—it could cooperate with other countries on the civilian-based defense policy itself, as discussed in the previous section. The transarmed country could promote an understanding of civilian-based defense. It could also share its knowledge and experience with other countries considering adopting civilian-based defense, as well as with those that had already begun the phased process of transarmament. The cooperation could later be continued in preparations and action to deal with crises.

In certain situations effective civilian-based defense preparations might inspire fear in a neighboring dictatorship that resistance know-how would spread to its own population. For example, during the long Polish crisis the Soviet Union has been deeply worried about the possible spread of the "Polish disease." If a dictatorship fearful of the spread of knowledge of how to resist were also threatened by a highly offensive political stance by the civilian-based defense coun-try, the dictatorship might invade to remove the source of constant irritation and political danger. (This situation is somewhat analogous to invasions provoked by a strong military build-up in a neighboring country.)

In case of such a pre-emptive invasion, the civilian-based defense country would be put to a severe test. If inadequately prepared, that country could be silenced or even crushed. If well prepared, the population—skilled and able to wage effective defense and to subvert the attackers' troops—could produce a débacle for the invader. The crisis could even trigger a civilian uprising at home and disintegrate the attacking regime. Something similar occurred with the Japanese military defeat of the Russian Empire, which was one of several causes of the 1905 Russian Revolution. That is optimistic, however, and all factors in such a situation need to be carefully examined.

An offensive political stance should not be combined with civilian-based defense unless the society has the strength and willingness to back it up under strong pressure or actual attack. Countries in espe-cially vulnerable political, economic, or geographical situations would generally be wiser to adopt a political posture closer to the defensive end of the spectrum in order not to provoke an invasion. Finland and (probably) Austria are such countries. If well prepared, Britain, France, and West Germany would be in stronger positions to take a more offensive political stance if they wished.

SOCIAL SYSTEM AND DEFENSE SYSTEM

Most Europeans are rightly proud of their democratic traditions and practices, and readily accept that they merit defense against all internal and foreign attacks. Some individuals strongly committed to one or another doctrine of radical social change have, however, argued that it is not possible to apply civilian-based defense until and unless a major societal transformation first occurs, a change which would break up major concentrations of economic and political power, or bring them under some kind of societal control or ownership. According to this view, only a society of great justice, whose institutions do not depend for their continuation on the threat or use of violence, can be defended nonviolently. Therefore, discussion of transarmament under present conditions is believed to be nonsense. However impressive their arguments may sometimes be, these individuals do not adequately recognize the relative merits of their present societies or the importance of preventing systems from being made worse by attackers as a prerequisite to improving society. Most importantly, they are not fully aware of the fact that improvised nonviolent struggle for defense has already been applied in highly imperfect societies.

Civilian-based defense does not require ideal social conditions for its adoption and practice, any more than does nonviolent struggle generally. Indeed, much improvised nonviolent action has occurred in societies ruled by elitist, oppressive, and dictatorial systems of either foreign or domestic origins. These societies often contained internal injustices, élite and class rule, ethnic and linguistic heterogeneity, and extreme social and political conflict. The opposite conditions—social harmony, diffused effective power, decentralization, and vibrant democracy—would be more conducive to the use and success of such action, but they are not prerequisites. This was demonstrated by the German Weimar Republic's official policies waging civilian noncooperation and defiance in 1920 against the Kapp 'Putsch' by pro-monarchist paramilitary groups, and against the 1923 Franco-Belgian invasion and occupation (both described in Chapter 2). Germany at the time was anything but a harmonious, egalitarian, violence-free society. It is therefore possible that highly imperfect societies can officially decide to defend themselves against aggressors by nonviolent forms of struggle, and that such resistance can be applied with powerful effect.

The way is therefore open for serious consideration and development of civilian-based defense by widely differing societies. All Western European societies could use this policy. The societies which adopt civilian-based defense may have very contrasting views of the sources of the threats against them. Some may fear, for example, invasion by the Soviet Union, some a coup d'état, and others an invasion supported by the United States.

This does not mean, however, that all governments and systems can be defended by civilian-based defense, without changes before or during the transarmament period or during the defense struggle itself. To take an extreme example, severe dictatorships which apply terror to rule a deeply alienated population ought not to expect an outpouring of popular support to defend that system. The people would lack the will to defend it, and the society's non-state institutions would lack the strength and resilience capable of repelling the attack.

Certain types of authoritarian regimes and societies might, however, experience changes before and even under attack which would enable them to apply nonviolent struggle. This is illustrated by the improvised Czechoslovak struggles against invasion and the Polish resistance to martial law. An authoritarian society might itself be reshaped by strong popular improvised defense against a foreign attack. This defense would be waged in support of the country, rather than of the regime. During such a crisis people would directly assume responsibility for defense and for the workings of the society, even creating new non-state institutions to meet social, economic, and political needs.

In other situations the authoritarian system might have been imposed, not to benefit a ruling élite, but to protect the society against foreign attack or foreign-instigated coups d'état intended to destroy the society's new social or economic changes or its recent social revolution. In such cases, civilian-based defense could provide another way to deter and defeat attacks, one compatible with internal democratization. If so, the adoption of the policy and shift to political freedom would depend on the élite's commitment to its avowed ideals or on an internal democratic change by popular action.

A long-term link does exist between the policy of civilian-based defense and "democracy"—that is, a political system with popular participation in decisionmaking.[8] Democratic participation in peacetime will help to increase the society's defense potential by this policy. Conversely, civilian-based defense will contribute to democratic participation and the diffusion of power—both avowed goals of diverse systems, including some now ruled by minority parties or idealistic élites.

RESPONSES TO TRANSARMAMENT

If the countries of Western Europe could achieve an effective deterrence and defense capability by their own efforts through the civilian-based defense policy, the United States should respond with relief and gratitude. That shift to self-reliance would significantly reduce the demands on the United States for military equipment, personnel, and financial resources. Simultaneously, the danger of an outbreak of nuclear war on that continent among the people and nations to which many in the United States feel most akin—would be significantly reduced or even virtually eliminated.

The Soviet Union, however, is most unlikely to be pleased with either the addition of a civilian-based defense component to the defense armories of any Western European countries or the full transarmament of any of them. Certainly the USSR has had considerable difficulties dealing with nonviolent struggle, in Czechoslovakia and Poland in particular. The ideological threat is also important. Both nonviolent struggle generally and civilian-based defense in particular challenge two principles of Leninism: concentration of control in the hands of an élite in command of the state apparatus and the central role and omnipotence of violence. The refutation of these both in theory and practice would be perceived as a most dangerous development.

This prediction of Soviet response to transarmament in Europe is not shared by all. Some persons contend that the USSR has no hostile military aims toward the countries of Western Europe. They see Soviet military preparations as defensively motivated only. They point to the immense number of Soviet casualties and tremendous destruction during the Second World War as a powerful stimulus for strong efforts to achieve world peace. These persons may also argue, with evidence, that the history of foreign military intervention, military alliances, and military bases directed against the USSR, as well as the targeting of nuclear weapons against Soviet cities and military bases, adequately explain Soviet military preparations and actions, even those seen by outsiders as aggressive—as the invasion of Afghanistan.

Also, some undemocratic aspects of Soviet society may be in part domestic consequences of foreign military dangers. Stalin maintained that the needs of military security were among the reasons why a workers' democracy was "impossible." To achieve the Communist ideal, he said, it was necessary to have "a completely secure, peaceful condition all round, so that we should not need large military cadres . . . which put their imprint on the other governmental institutions. . . ."[9]

If any of those more tolerant perspectives on Soviet policies is valid, transarmament by individual European countries or by the North Atlantic alliance—or even only the replacement of nuclear weapons to deter a Soviet invasion with civilian-based defense preparations alongside conventional forces—could reduce or remove Soviet fears of Western military attack. That might then contribute to a reduction of the Soviet military effort and potentially help relax internal political controls.

Whatever may be the Soviet response to transarmament in Western Europe, however, the Eastern Europeans would have been brought new grounds for hope. The reduction of the Western military capacity would reduce pressures to maintain domestic submission within the Soviet bloc encouraged by the perceived danger of Western military attack. The growth of knowledge of nonviolent struggle, added to their own extensive experience, could encourage and aid the continuing efforts of Eastern Europeans to achieve self-liberation.

The peoples of the countries of Western Europe could celebrate some genuine progress, since a major start would have been made toward reducing the danger of nuclear and massive conventional war, and toward making their societies unconquerable by any aggressor or would-be dictator. In the decades to come their societies would be the better for that change.

However, this is neither a risk-free path nor an easy one. Those who take it bear a heavy responsibility, which continues indefinitely, to maintain the vigilance, preparations, and courage necessary to ensure the survival of liberty and human dignity.

4 PREVENTING ATTACK

CIVILIAN-BASED DETERRENCE AND DEFENSE

The major objective of civilian-based defense is to prevent potential internal and foreign attackers from launching any hostile action. Adoption of a defense policy which lacks a military attack capacity would eliminate the motive for a pre-emptive attack by neighbors fearful of being attacked themselves. Likelihood of attack can also be reduced or eliminated by foreign and domestic policies that promote understanding, respect, and goodwill. However, certain hostile regimes and groups may be unmoved by those policies and may even interpret them as weaknesses inviting an invasion or an internal takeover. Neither an absence of provocation nor neutrality guarantees safety from foreign attacks. Therefore, some form of deterrence capacity is still required, in addition to other means of dissuasion.

We have become so accustomed to thinking in terms of nuclear deterrence or massively destructive conventional military capacity that it is difficult at times to understand how the very different means employed in civilian-based defense—which do not threaten massive physical destruction and annihilation—can deter potential attackers. We will understand this better if we think about the forces influencing the decisions of those contemplating an invasion or internal usurpation in light of an understanding of the power potential of civilian-based defense.

As was discussed in Chapter 1, "deterrence" is a broader concept than military or nuclear deterrence. Deterrence occurs when potential attackers have decided not to commit a hostile act because consequences which they prefer to avoid would follow. The ability to deny the objectives of an attack and to impose unacceptable costs can produce deterrence whether the denial and costs result from violent or nonviolent actions.

Internal usurpations and foreign invasions are rarely, if ever, ends in themselves. They are intended to achieve certain objectives. Both are therefore likely to be rationally calculated acts. If it is expected that the objectives will be gained easily and the costs will be small, the attack may be launched. On the other hand, if the objectives are unlikely to be gained and the anticipated costs are excessive, then, although the goal may still be desired, the attack is likely to be postponed or abandoned. It will have been deterred.

Political control of the country is crucial to gaining the objectives of both invaders and internal usurpers. They usually realize that. Therefore, barring a huge gamble or pure irrationality, the likelihood of failure in establishing political control is likely to deter potential attackers. Other factors which also may contribute to deterrence include unacceptable anticipated economic, ideological, domestic, and international costs of the attack, and the prospect of the attackers' own trooops and functionaries becoming unreliable and of their aggressive actions being ineffective.

Whether, and to what degree, civilian-based defense can provide deterrence in a specific situation depends on three factors: the actual capability of the society relying on civilian-based defense (1) to deny the attackers their objectives; (2) to impose (alone or in cooperation with others) unacceptable costs; and (3) the perception by the potential attackers of the society's capability to do (1) and (2).

A shift to civilian-based defense makes possible a reunion of deterrence and defense. In pre-nuclear times it was the ability to defend successfully which deterred attacks. Nuclear weapons deter by the prospect of annihilation, precluding the ability to defend. Now, once again, deterrence can be produced by the capacity to defend.

In contrast to past improvised nonviolent struggles, the population of a country with a prepared civilian-based defense capacity will be in a state of readiness to defend against attempted take-overs and invasions. The population will be prepared to fulfil the three basic requirements for effective deterrence.

First, the attackers' objectives must be denied. To do this, resistance is required on two fronts: (1) Legitimacy must be denied to the attackers, collaboration prevented, and establishment of effective control blocked. The society must maintain political noncooperation with the usurpers on a massive scale, while it retains self-direction and loyalty to its own principles and system. (2) The attackers' wider objectives (economic, ideological, political and other) must also be directly resisted. The result of these struggles on both fronts is that few gains accrue to the attackers, while their costs escalate.

Second, the attackers' costs must be increased to an unacceptable level. The international costs will vary with the situation, but they can include serious economic, diplomatic, and prestige losses. Their domestic costs could include heavy demands on economic resources, personnel, and administration for use in the attacked country. These are likely to reduce the ability to meet human and social needs at home. Domestic costs may also include loss of the regime's legitimacy—its population's belief in its right to rule—among its home population. At times that loss may lead to open dissent and opposition at home as well as in the attacked country. To these problems should be added possible morale and discipline problems among the regime's troops and functionaries, which may have been aggravated by the defenders' efforts to induce disaffection among them.

Finally, if potential attackers are to be deterred by civilian-based defense preparations, they must understand realistically that they are likely to be denied both their objectives and political control and also that their costs will be unacceptably high. They must see that they would very probably lose.

To sharpen that perception, the nature of a civilian-based defense policy, its capacities, and preparations and training for it should, generally speaking, be publicized. It would be important to communicate to all possible attackers an accurate perception of the defensive capability of the country prepared with this policy. Possible attackers may learn about the power potential of civilian-based defense through: the publicly available information concerning general plans, preparations, and training (as publications, films, handbooks, news stories, and the like); reports and observations of particular large-scale training and exercises, such as maneuvers (acting out on a city or regional level defense plans against hypothetical attackers); international conferences on the policy (as under the auspices of a division of the United Nations); and direct public and government-to-government communications and warnings.

DETERRING INTERNAL USURPATIONS

At present there is no adequate policy for deterring coups d'état and similar internal usurpations. The threat of military action is inadequate. Indeed, coups are usually carried out by some part of the military forces themselves (which are supposed to defend the system) or by a political group with the submission or inaction of the police and military forces. In country after country the regular constitutional procedures have been inadequate to deter and defeat such attacks. Other means are therefore needed. Civilian-based defense might provide those means.

Coups and executive usurpations are not automatically successful when the government buildings, transportation centers, communication offices, and other facilities have been seized. It is also necessary for the usurpers to achieve political consolidation and control over the governmental apparatus, the population, and the society's institutions.[1]

Widespread confusion, a desire to avoid conflict, a mood of "wait-and-see," a sense of powerlessness, ignorance of how to resist: all greatly assist the usurpers to achieve the political consolidation and domination they need. The preparations and training for civilian-based defense are designed to prevent precisely that situation. In addition to coups, more subtle attempts at usurpation—as an unnecessary "state of emergency"—may also be identified and thwarted by a prepared populace. Denial of legitimacy, refusal of obedience, and noncooperation by the general populace, by the societal institutions, and by the branches of government and their employees can effectively prevent the political consolidation and control that make a usurpation successful. The resulting political paralysis might also be accompanied by efforts to induce the usurpers' troops and functionaries to abandon the attempt and to resume loyalty to the legitimate government. That combination could effectively dissolve the coup. This actually occurred in the French resistance to the 1961 generals' 'Putsch' in Algiers (as described in Chapter 2).[2]

Preparations to resist internal usurpations should include establishment of a moral and legal obligation of the citizens to refuse to cooperate with such attacks, and specific training for resistance by civil servants, police, communications employees, military personnel (where full transarmament has not occurred), members of the society's institutions, and the general populace.

Advance knowledge of that prepared resistance capacity and an accurate perception of its power could deter internal usurpations. For this type of attack, simply the probability of failure to consolidate control over both the state machinery and the general society would cause most would-be usurpers to abandon the idea.

DETERRING FOREIGN INVASIONS

Invasions also can be deterred by the perceived ability of a society to deny invaders their objectives and to impose unacceptable costs. Even ruthless tyrants, if they face power realities, may be deterred by a society that can block their goals and inflict extreme costs. Few tyrants would attack a politically indigestible society that might subvert their own regime. This applies to a possible Soviet invasion of Western European countries.

First, even when not confronting civilian-based defense preparations, potential invaders and occupiers must contemplate the major practical requirements of their possible aggression. These include the needed financial resources, equipment, administrative capacity, and personnel. Even the normal difficulties of attempting to rule occupied countries are immense. George F. Kennan has reminded us of the general difficulties in establishing and maintaining control over large areas and populations:

> Many Americans seem unable to recognize the technical difficulties involved in the operation of far-flung lines of power—the difficulty of trying to exert power from any given national center, over areas greatly remote from that center. There are, believe me, limits to the effective radius of political power from any center in the world. It is vitally important to remember this, particularly in face of the fears one hears constantly expressed today that the Russians want universal power and will be likely to take over the world if we fail to do this or that.
>
> There is no magic by which great nations are brought to obey for any length of time the will of people very far away who understand their problems poorly and with whom they feel no intimacy of origin or understanding. This has to be done by bayonets, or it is not done at all. . . .

What I am asserting is that universal world domination is a technical impossibility, and that the effectiveness of the power radiated from any one national center decreases in proportion to the distance involved, and to the degree of cultural disparity.[3]

It is possible that such difficulties already would confront a Soviet attempt to occupy Western Europe to a degree sufficient to constitute a significant deterrent. Large-scale preparations and training for civilian-based defense would vastly multiply the normal difficulties and problems encountered by foreign occupation regimes. A major part of the difficulties attackers would face in attempting to counter prepared civilian-based defense is associated with the nonviolent character of civilian-based defense. When nonviolent struggle is consciously applied, the attackers cannot rely on the common assumption that the threat and use of military action and repression will induce passive submission. Knowledgeable practitioners of nonviolent struggle understand that victory often requires that the populace continue resistance despite casualties. When violence is applied against the civilian defenders, the spirit of defiance may remain, and the attackers' violence may prove to be counterproductive. It may increase resistance, arouse third party support, and even stimulate splits in the attackers' own camp. This process is called "political 'jiu-jitsu.'"[4] An understanding of it by the potential invaders will greatly increase the deterrent effect of civilian-based defense.

The would-be occupiers may well find it to their advantage not to attempt to bring under their control people actively opposed to their regime, determined to defeat it, and thoroughly trained in a technique that can be used to do so. That spirit of resistance could well spread to other countries under the invaders' regime, and even to their own people and troops. The methods used by the defending population could be copied and multiplied, and applied against the tyranny in the invaders' homeland. The prospect of these results of an attack would not encourage potential invaders. Where vigilance and the active practice of democracy are reinforced by an effective, well-prepared means of defense, the chances of invasion will be significantly reduced.

Could such a civilian-based defense capacity deter potential attackers in Western Europe? Could it deter the Soviet Union if it wanted to invade and occupy Western European countries? Let us explore these questions. They are important and ought not to be considered lightly. For various reasons, the political system of the Soviet Union is probably less responsive to external influences than the systems of any other potential attackers. Also, the Soviet military forces are significantly larger than those readily available to any other possible invaders. Therefore, if civilian-based defense capacity could deter the Soviet Union, it most likely could deter any other state.

Examination of the potential of civilian-based defense to deter a possible Soviet military sweep westward is not based on paranoia. Soviet behavior to its Western neighbors has not always been exemplary. Major parts of Finland were ceded to the Soviet Union following the Winter War of 1939–1940, which began with a Soviet attack. Following the 1939 agreement between Nazi Germany and the Soviet Union to divide Poland between them, Soviet troops invaded from the east to seize the half left for them by the Nazi invaders from the west. The Soviet military and political dominance in Eastern Europe since 1945 has been rooted in the course and aftermath of the Second World War, in which the Eastern European countries had been either occupied by Nazi Germany following invasion or allied with it. It is true that the motive for the Soviet invasions of those countries was to defeat Nazi Germany, not territorial aggrandizement. However, the military occupations of those countries were then used to place indigenous Communist parties in control of the state apparatuses, often with leaders trained during the war in the Soviet Union. Latvia, Lithuania, and Estonia were annexed outright.

Several reasons why the Soviet Union might invade and occupy Western European countries were suggested in Chapter 1. Should the Soviet Union be interested in doing so, there are good grounds to expect that those countries which had transarmed to civilian-based defense could effectively deter the attack.

First, the Soviet experiences in maintaining the political fruits of their military conquests have been sobering. Popular unrest against Communist rule in Eastern Europe following the Second World War took only a few years to manifest itself. The first case was the predominantly nonviolent East German Rising of June 16-17, 1953. Later there occurred the Polish protests of 1956 and the Hungarian Revolution of 1956–1957. These were followed by the Czechoslovak liberalization in the spring and summer of 1968 and the nonviolent struggle against the Soviet and Warsaw Pact invasion and occupation from August 1968 to April 1969. Protests and strikes occurred in Poland in 1968, 1970–1971 and 1976. The democratization in Poland by Solidarity and related organizations in 1980–1981, the struggle against martial law after December 1981, and later resistance have done more to dismantle dictatorial Communist rule than anything the Pentagon has accomplished. That is remarkable, since improvised struggle under an existing Communist dictatorship is more difficult than prepared struggle by a trained population—a characteristic of civilian-based defense.

All of these struggles have shaken Communist rule and Soviet hegemony. In the most important cases the Soviet troops sent to repress the nonviolent popular struggles experienced severe morale problems, and some soldiers and officers disobeyed orders and mutinied.[5] There have been reports, for example, that the Soviet troops which initially invaded and occupied Czechoslovakia in 1968 became sufficiently unreliable within a few days that they had to be sent back to the Soviet Union and replaced by non-Russian-speaking troops, with whom the Czechs and Slovaks could not easily communicate.[6]

In Poland in 1980 and 1981 the Soviet troops would have faced an even more sophisticated and widespread nonviolent resistance. It is more than a negligible possibility that the lesson of 1968—that the Soviet troops were highly vulnerable to this special kind of combat— was a contributing factor in the decision not to send them into Poland. That meant, of course, relying on the Polish Army instead to act against Solidarity. That, too, was risky. Calculations must have been made that as along as the Soviet Army stayed out, the Polish troops would obey orders. If not, a Soviet invasion remained an option. Investigation and analysis of why the Polish troops obeyed in that situation, and under what conditions they might not have done so or might not do so in the future, are clearly required. Whatever the reasons, however, it remains true that Soviet troops were not used, despite the fact that, from the perspective of the Kremlin leaders, the Polish situation was far more serious than that in Czechoslovakia in 1968. While speculation can be dangerous, it can also point to important questions that otherwise might not be asked, which in turn could lead to significant new information.

Civilian-based defense theorists have in earlier literature projected that following an invasion, once the foreign troops are in the country, it might be possible deliberately to induce disaffection, unreliability, and even mutiny among the attackers' troops and functionaries. If that occurred, it would strongly affect the actual defense struggle. However, unless the potential attackers seriously expected in advance that this might result from ordering their troops to re-press nonviolent resisters, the possibility would not increase the deterrence capacity of the policy. No one in the literature has until now suggested the possibility of destroying the reliability, discipline, and even participation of the attackers' troops in advance of an attack, during preparations for an invasion. No known historical case had suggested that possibility.

That possibility is suggested, however, by the reported actions of Soviet army reservists in the southern Carpathian Military District along the Polish border when they were mobilized in August-December 1980.[7] The reservists were called up for refresher training and other preparations for possible invasion of Poland and occupation duty there. Soviet invasion preparations reached a peak of readiness in December 1980 and again in March 1981.[8] The 1980 mobilization reportedly encountered very serious discipline problems. Conse-quently, by mid-December the reservists in the Carpathian Military District were already being deactivated and returned to their usual civilian jobs.[9] Kevin Klose reported in 'The Washington Post' that "reliable sources" indicated that the August mobilization of reserv-ists in the region "was marked by extraordinary confusion, disorder and wholesale desertions by reservists from mustering points and bivouacs." The events led to "dismissal of senior staff reservists re-sponsible for reserve readiness in the Carpathian region." Reservists had been told they were going for "retraining," and it is not known what they may or may not have known about the relation of this to events in Poland. Soviet sources reported, Klose continued, that from the start discipline among the recalled reservists was a major problem.

> These sources alleged that the reservists, with families and friends nearby, melted away from their duties in numbers so large that punishment became impossible. They cited persistent insubordination, low morale and poor per-formance as major problems. These were said to have been major factors lead-ing to the order to disband.[10]

On the basis of Soviet sources, Richard D. Anderson, Jr., writing in 'Problems of Communism', indicated that plant managers and medical personnel may have provided the reservists with excuses that they should not be called to active duty because they were needed in the factory or because their health was not good. He also offered evidence that lack of coordination between military commanders and local civilian authorities may explain why deserting reservists were not punished.[11]

The Carpathian insubordinations and desertions may have strengthened the hand of President Brezhnev, who reportedly was opposed to invading Poland, against military officers and those Politburo members who favored military action, especially Communist Party Secretary Andrei Kirilenko. If the Carpathian reports are true, Anderson wrote, this explains the resurgence of Brezhnev's influence after the decision to mobilize, which he reportedly also had discouraged. "The troubles [during mobilization] would strengthen the hand of political leaders opposed to invasion, since the Soviet army's ability to defeat Polish resistance would be lowered if its troops were unreliable. The troubles would also discredit some advocates of invasion." [12]

Whatever the additional details of this case and the motives for the reservists' actions, these events suggest the wisdom of a civilian-based defense country taking steps to encourage a positive and sympathetic understanding of its people and way of life among the general population and military personnel of potential attacking regimes. This could make their population and troops less likely to support or participate in an invasion, thereby helping to deter it.

The potential deterrent effect of possible direct Polish nonviolent struggle against a Soviet invasion and occupation is unknown. However, the question was clearly considered in Moscow, since a writer in 'Pravda' on 5 December 1980 argued that such resistance could be surmounted. He proposed, Anderson reported, "that those who refused to work be dealt with by the time-tested methods of reduced food rations and assignment to manual labor." The 'Pravda' writer thereby implied, in Anderson's words, that Lech Walesa's threats of nonviolent resistance "could be handled and thus need not deter Soviet action." [13] (Note that the 'Pravda' writer did not place confidence in naked military action to end strikes and slowdowns!)

Much more limited nonviolent struggles and demonstrations have occurred earlier within the Soviet Union itself. These may have helped the regime to understand the potential power of nonviolent struggle, hence assisting its future deterrent effect in prepared forms. The past cases include strikes in the prison labor camps (especially Vorkuta) in 1953, the demonstrations by civil rights advocates and by Jews seeking to emigrate, and the hunger strikes by Dr. Andrei Sakharov, his wife, Dr. Yelena Bonner, and others.

With this experience, the much more extensive use of nonviolent struggle in Eastern Europe, and with its own internal problems, the

Soviet Union would likely be very cautious about any proposal to invade and occupy countries with populations highly motivated, well prepared, and carefully trained to defend their societies, defeat attackers, and subvert occupation troops and functionaries. The spirit and knowledge of this type of resistance could well spread to other countries under Soviet rule or hegemony and to the peoples and troops of the USSR. The Soviet Union's political and economic difficulties, and the linguistic, ethnic, and nationality diversity of its population provide potentially fertile grounds for the spread of this type of action. The erosion of faith in the official ideology and the desires of youth and intellectuals for greater liberties provide additional minds hungry for ideas about "what is to be done." The methods used by the defending population, the idea of freedom, and the knowledge of how to struggle for it effectively could be brought back home. There, in time, that idea and that knowledge might grow into an uncontrollable force, even dwarfing the liberation movement in Poland. Any competent Soviet leadership is unlikely to expose itself to these dangers by invading a single civilian-based defense country, much less several Western European countries armed with this policy. The more countries attacked, and the more extensive and higher quality the defense preparations in those countries, the heavier would be the demands on the invaders' system and the greater the difficulties of maintaining control and achieving the attackers' objectives.

Without the advantage of such past experience, and without other sources of strategic sophistication about nonviolent struggle, the rulers of hostile states might initially seriously miscalculate. The prospect of invading a country without military capacity might at first appear to the potential attackers to be an easy venture, with certain success and little cost. Attention might be simplistically focussed on the fact that resistance would not include either military combat at the frontier or military retaliation.

However, that view would most likely change if the potential attackers' political and military leaders examined seriously the defenders' preparations and the general capabilities of civilian-based defense. A careful calculation of the requirements and the costs of the attack and the chances of gaining the objectives would be likely to force a serious reevaluation of any invasion proposal, and possibly its cancellation. The earlier view which dismissed the capacity of

Table Two. Comparative Deterrence.

Deterrence Policy	Success	Failure	Possible Consequences of Failure of Deterrence
Nuclear	No attack	Nuclear war	Massive destruction and dangers of annihilation
Civilian-based defense	No attack	Defense policy implemented	Defeat and life under harsh dictatorial rule or Successful defense with free way of life restored

civilian-based defense might then be recognized as strategic self-deception by officials who had not taken the unorthodox defense plans seriously.

Careful examination of the power potential of the defenders' preparations would make it apparent that the prospect of easy entry of troops into the civilian-based country would be simply the initial stage of a political ambush, from which invading forces could escape only through a major political disaster. Potential attackers of civilian-based defense countries would have to prepare well, perhaps more so than against militarily defended societies. They would have to consider not only the requirements for the initial attack, but also those for an effective long-term occupation. Potential attackers would also have to examine ways to counteract and defeat continuing defense struggles in the occupied, but not defeated, country. Facing that prospect, the leaders of the potential aggressor state are unlikely to order an attack. A significant deterrence capacity therefore exists in civilian-based defense. As with all deterrence policies it is not foolproof, and an invasion might even then be launched. In this case, the result is not massive destruction, as with the failure of nuclear deterrence, but the application of the defense policy itself, as shown in Table Two on comparative deterrence.

In light of the reality that various of the international dangers are related to nuclear weapons, it is important now to examine possible ways that civilian-based defense might help prevent nuclear attacks.

DISSUADING NUCLEAR ATTACKS

With a civilian-based defense policy, nuclear weapons are unnecessary and even counterproductive, for they create threats to national security and survival. This is true whether nuclear weapons are provided by an alliance, are based in the country by an ally, or are independently controlled. If a country adopts civilian-based defense against conventional invasions and ends association with nuclear weapons and bases, two of the most serious dangers of nuclear attack are removed: pre-emptive strike to prevent an expected nuclear attack and escalation of a conventional war to a nuclear one.

As we have noted earlier, when a country directly possesses nuclear weapons, or provides bases for them, or even belongs to a nuclear alliance (hence bringing suspicion of regular or emergency basing), it becomes virtually inevitable that opposing nuclear powers will target that country. Deployment of nuclear weapons, or assistance in such deployment, makes a country extremely dangerous to others, whatever the actual intent. That country will be seen as a potential attacker or accomplice to a nuclear attack.

On the other hand, countries which do not possess nuclear weapons, have no nuclear bases, and are not members of a nuclear alliance, minimize the likelihood of being targeted by other nuclear powers. Zaire, Colombia, New Zealand, Sri Lanka, and Morocco do not seriously expect nuclear attack. The United States, the Soviet Union, China, Britain, France, and the countries with nuclear bases or with facilities that might be used in nuclear war do contemplate seriously the possibility of nuclear attack. They claim their nuclear capacity, or that of their alliance, is required to deter potential attacks. In fact, that capacity is a major stimulus of the danger.

Transarmament to civilian-based defense, in contrast, drastically reduces the likelihood of being targeted and pre-emptively attacked.[14]

Civilian-based defense can also reduce the danger of escalation of a conflict to nuclear war. This danger exists under both present NATO policies and the proposals to shift from nuclear deterrence for Western European security to an expanded conventional military capacity for NATO and for individual countries. Within the framework of military means, there is always the possibility that one side or another, fearing defeat, would resort to nuclear weapons—acquired from an ally, kept in hidden stocks, or freshly assembled. The danger is most acute under present conditions, in which both alliances are tied to dominant nuclear powers.

By replacing conventional military weaponry and nuclear weapons with civilian-based defense, the defense struggle could be kept entirely outside the military framework. This would virtually eliminate the danger of escalation to nuclear war. Nor is a nuclear attack on the country with a nonmilitary defense policy likely as a means of securing political or other goals. The normal goals of invasions—political, economic, ideological, and territorial—could not be achieved and would even be directly endangered by the use of nuclear weapons in the territory to be occupied. A nuclear attack at the beginning of an invasion would therefore be counterproductive for the attackers. Once civilian-based defense is under way against an invasion and occupation, the presence of the attackers' personnel in the country would drastically reduce or eliminate any large-scale use of nuclear weapons.

Even on the scale of Hiroshima and Nagasaki, selective atomic attacks on a civilian-based defense country to induce political submission would be tragic. However, the small likelihood of their occurring and the relatively limited scale of the resulting destruction and casualties need to be compared with the results of the significantly larger nuclear attacks to which nuclear powers or nuclear-base countries might be subjected.

The potential for small-scale use of nuclear weapons for pure destruction or vindictive punishment of the defiant population exists, but it is doubtful that it would occur, for four reasons. First, once the civilian-based defense struggles are under way, the dynamics of the conflict strongly tend to shift the attackers' measures away from the more blatant forms of violence and toward efforts to gain political control. This clearly occurred, for example, in Czechoslovakia within a few days in August 1968 and extended well into the next year, even beyond the ascent of Gustav Husak to leadership in April.

Second, in some cases people in the attackers' homeland, repelled by a nuclear attack against a nonviolent population, may react disruptively. Where news can reach the general population, the regime may suffer a general loss of legitimacy and support, while having to deal with unrest and demonstrations. In addition, even if public knowledge can be restricted and delayed, this use of nuclear weapons

may be used by rival factions within the ruling élite to oust and replace the existing rulers.[15]

Third, the use of nuclear weapons against a civilian-based defense
country is likely to provoke serious international reactions. While
some states may be relatively indifferent to world opinion, hostility
and denunciations may nevertheless have an impact when accom-
panying diplomatic and economic sanctions threaten significant
international political and economic losses. In the case of nuclear
aggression, the greatly intensified revulsion is likely to mean that
such losses may be more widespread and lasting than is commonly
the case with international sanctions. The increasing dependence of
the Soviet Union and other countries on foreign trade and food ship-
ments increases the seriousness with which the prospect of international sanctions will be viewed.

Fourth, because the weather and winds generally move from west
to east in Europe, the Soviet Union would also have to take special
measures to prevent unacceptable nuclear fallout from Western
Europe from reaching Eastern Europe and the Soviet Union. Such
steps as using "clean" bombs or aerial explosions, or setting limits on
the explosions could reduce this danger to the USSR itself. However,
Soviet officials would need to be cautious about such actions. Awareness of them might lead the Soviet or Eastern European populations
to become alarmed and protest.

All these factors make a nuclear attack on a Western European
civilian-based defense country unlikely.

However, just as it is necessary to face the consequences of nuclear
war resulting from the failure of nuclear deterrence, so it is necessary to face the question of what a civilian-based defense country
would do under threat of nuclear attack—an extremely improbable
eventuality.

Various responses to implied or explicit threats should be examined. These should include diverse options, even an apparent bending
to specific demands at the moment, so as to be able later to regain
the political initiative. More defiant options are, however, potentially appropriate. If the threat had been made quietly through diplomatic channels, in order to induce some type of submission, then a
major publicity and diplomatic campaign could be launched, with
the aim of producing sufficient world revulsion and possibly domestic reactions in the attackers' homeland to block implementation of

the threat. A prudent nonviolent position in face of such threats would be to refuse to bow even to nuclear blackmail. Submission to a particular threat would likely be the beginning of a series with escalating demands, with no end in sight.[16] Refusal to submit to even nuclear threats is part of present NATO policy as well, except that in it the refusal to bow is combined with the threat of a NATO avenging counterattack, with the virtual certainty of a Soviet preemptive or retaliatory major nuclear strike. In order to reduce or eliminate nuclear threats and attacks from hostile ruthless states, it is essential in civilian-based defense that potential attackers be made aware that even those threats will not achieve their objectives.

It is highly unlikely but conceivable that in an unusual situation a hostile foreign state might hope to tyrannize a civilian-based defense country into submission by actual selective use of atomic weapons. However horrendous that prospect may be, it must be compared to what would happen if nuclear deterrence failed: probable massive nuclear attacks to eliminate second strike capability. With civilian-based defense, the absence of nuclear retaliation would most likely prevent the rapid escalation to nuclear devastation that is probable when both sides possess nuclear weapons.

If the civilian-based defense country had been attacked selectively with nuclear weapons to induce submission, the attackers would need to suspend such bombing to determine if it had produced the desired result. That pause would provide time for the outbreak of the domestic and international repercussions discussed above and for possible reassessment by the attackers of their strategy. Much greater chances would then exist for a cessation of nuclear attacks than would be the case when nuclear retaliation followed the first nuclear attack.

Civil defense measures against fallout from such limited attacks would make much more sense than against more massive nuclear attacks, for non-nuclear countries can survive limited small-scale nuclear attacks—as did Japan.[17] Civil defense measures need to be examined carefully in this context, since limited attacks differ significantly from the annihilation likely to result from attack and counterattack between two nuclear powers. In a civilian-based defense country, civil defense preparations become another part of a purely defensive posture. This contrasts with the perception of a large civil defense program in a major nuclear country as part of preparation for a first strike on its rival.[18]

Within the context of civilian-based defense, and beyond civil defense efforts, attention should also be given to the desirability and potential effectiveness of developing and deploying purely defensive technological measures against nuclear attacks (whether in the anti-ballistic missile form or some other). Work would be required on the likely effectiveness of such measures and their relative contribution to security, as compared with other means, alongside the civilian-based defense policy. It could be difficult to demonstrate that such research, development, and deployment were purely defensive, and that would be necessary to preclude a pre-emptive attack. (Such an attack could be based on the false belief that the defensive anti-ballistic missiles were actually disguised offensive nuclear-armed rockets.)

In summary, while civilian-based defense is not directly a deterrent against nuclear attack, the policy can by other forces of dissuasion significantly reduce the chances of such a catastrophe. The strictly defensive nature of the policy would, if accurately perceived, remove the fears which could produce pre-emptive attacks and dangerous steps of military escalation which could lead also to a nuclear attack. Recognition that this was a policy of people sufficiently strong that they did not require the threat of mutual annihilation in order to refuse to submit to nuclear blackmail could also reduce the incidence of such threats. The choice of a strictly defensive policy to deal with security threats combined with a foreign policy concerned with human rights and welfare throughout the world could contribute to a reservoir of international goodwill which also would discourage attacks. In other words, the nonoffensive nature of civilian-based defense and its other political and international influences tend strongly to dissuade massively destructive attacks by nuclear or other means.

Major work is needed to examine and evaluate such possible dissuasive effects of transarmament on the probability of nuclear attack. It is important to learn how to maximize these effects while securing a society's principles, independence, and survival. In addition, both negotiated and self-reliant ways of reducing nuclear dangers need to be continually and fully explored.

WHAT IF DETERRENCE FAILS?

For Europe itself, transarmament to civilian-based defense potentially provides a way to reduce the dangers of the continent becoming a nuclear wasteland. It could do this by providing strong means of deterring and defending against a Soviet conventional invasion without the threat or use of nuclear weapons. Deterrence by civilian-based defense of such an attack is rooted in the capacity of the society with this policy to defend itself successfully, and to defeat the attackers' efforts to gain control and specific objectives. An understanding of how the policy works to achieve defense against actual attack is needed to appreciate the deterrence potential of civilian-based defense. It is therefore important to examine more fully in the next two chapters how this policy could provide effective defense.

That topic is important for another reason as well. No deterrent—military or civilian—can ever be guaranteed to deter. Capacity to deal with its possible failure is therefore essential. The requirements, conditions, and risks of deterrence by civilian-based defense need to be fairly compared with those of deterrence by present conventional military and nuclear policies. The consequences of failure of deterrence by each policy must also be compared, along with the courses of defensive or remedial action which can then be taken. This is almost never done.

Table Two is designed to facilitate comparison of nuclear and civilian-based deterrence of invasion. Many people compare the best possible results of nuclear weapons—successful deterrence ("no attack")—with the worst possible results of civilian-based defense—failure of both its deterrence and defense capabilities, and therefore "harsh dictatorial rule." This is, of course, not a reasonable comparison. Success and failure of each policy for deterrence, as well as of the respective consequences of the failure of the two deterrence policies, need to be compared with each other, as the table indicates.

Unlike failure of nuclear deterrence, the failure of civilian-based defense preparations to deter invasion of Western Europe does not bring likelihood of annihilation, but instead application for the first time of the real defense capacity.

5 IN FACE OF ATTACK

CLOSE ENCOUNTER DEFENSE

Neither an attempted coup d'état nor even the physical occupation of the country by foreign troops signifies defeat. Not only does human life continue and hope for victory remain, but at this point the struggle enters a new active stage with a direct confrontation of forces. The defense struggle itself begins.

Apart from deterrence of some type and the broader influences of dissuasion, nothing that now exists can keep attacking forces and weapons from crossing the frontier. It is almost never recognized that this is true of modern military means as well as of civilian-based defense. The old idea of a conventional military defense at the frontiers to protect the homeland and its people has not been possible since at least the First World War. The changes in military technology—which made possible massive bombardments of defense lines, tank warfare, bombing by airplanes, and delivery of explosives by rockets—abolished the capacity of frontal warfare to protect the homeland from destruction and the civilian population from massive deaths. Military warfare is often still used in attempts to achieve defense at the frontier, but it has only the most dubious prospects of success. Indeed, military warfare for defense today almost universally guarantees that the homeland and the civilian population will suffer massively as the enemy strikes at the home base of the war effort.

In contrast with this, civilian-based defense does not attempt defense at the frontier, except occasional, largely symbolic, actions designed to communicate a will to resist. In civilian-based defense the invasion forces are allowed, as in an ambush, to enter the country in order to engage them in struggle at closer range in ways more likely to defeat them without the massive casualties and destruction of military warfare.

Civilian-based defense is the direct defense of society as such—its principles, free institutions, and liberties—rather than a futile attempt to defend territory as an indirect means to defend the society. When successful, civilian-based defense of the society would lead to the collapse of the internal usurpers or the withdrawal of the invaders. That result would follow from the successful direct defense of the society, not from struggle aimed at the control of terrain.

The period of close encounter defense is certain to require sacrifice and suffering—as with any technique of open struggle against tyrants and aggressors. The conflict may also, however, help to strengthen freedom and undermine tyranny far beyond the limits of the immediate contest because it will teach, by example, lessons in how people can act effectively to achieve those ends.

It is difficult for many people to understand how civilian-based defense can wield effective power against invaders or internal usurpers. This is largely because most people lack knowledge of both past improvised nonviolent campaigns and of the effectiveness added by preparations for such struggle. First, the history of past cases of nonviolent struggle in extreme conflicts is generally little known. Unfamiliarity with the relevant historical record makes it possible for many people to maintain their faith that military options are superior to all others, and also their certainty that intimidation and brutalities by dictatorships are omnipotent unless superior violence can be wielded against them. Second, as a prepared policy—based on research, feasibility studies, various types of preparation, and training—civilian-based defense differs from the past improvised cases. The new prepared policy is projected by its analysts to be more effective than the earlier cases, but it is not easy for people new to the subject to grasp this.

Our ability to evaluate this policy's potential will be increased by more understanding of past improvised cases, the nature of nonviolent struggle, problems of occupations and usurpers, weaknesses of dictatorships, strategies for civilian-based defense, and examination of the role of research, preparations, and training in improving effectiveness. Studies of how this policy might be applied for meeting the defense needs of particular countries are also necessary. These feasibility studies for particular countries are high priorities, but they are unlikely to be a suitable basis for judgments on the general applicability of civilian-based defense in other situations. Studies of the impact of noncooperation on diverse political systems are needed to assist that broader evaluation.

Most of this chapter and the next will take the form of a generalized scenario to help us to understand how a prepared society could use civilian-based defense against foreign aggression and internal takeovers. This discussion will focus on the basic dynamics likely to operate in these contingencies and the likely main components and stages of such struggles.[1] From this exploration we can gain insights into the policy's application to meet the various defense and security needs of Western European countries.

This attempt to sketch how an as yet undeveloped defense policy can combat attackers has had few military counterparts. New weapons of war and whole new weapons systems—rifles, dynamite, machine guns, tanks, airplanes, rockets, nuclear weapons, and the like—have been invented by individuals, groups, and governments, and then adopted by military forces and governments without thorough feasibility studies of their utility and long-term consequences. Even pioneering analyses of the future potential of new weapons, such as the writings about tank warfare by Sir Basil Liddell Hart in the 1930s, came well after the invention and adoption of the weapons themselves.[2]

Even without the recommended study and advance planning of civilian-based defense, it is possible that simply the increased use of improvised nonviolent struggle against tyrannies and attacks will gradually but fundamentally alter the nature of defense policies.

Czechoslovakia 1968–1969 is an example of this increased use of nonviolent struggle for defense. In that case there was more widespread and early nonviolent noncooperation and defiance against the invasion itself and during the initial stage of occupation than have occurred in previous historical cases. In those a significant delay had usually existed before the mobilization of significant resistance. The continuing improvised struggle in Poland also has great defense significance that is yet to be analyzed.

While major advances are being made in improvised struggles, it is at this point wiser not to rely solely on them but to think and plan ahead. It is better to examine the potential of nonviolent struggle generally and of civilian-based defense in particular to enable us to determine, first, whether we wish to move in that direction. Then, if we do, that examination will help us to control and shape that move.

To implement civilian-based defense, people must have the will to prepare well, to struggle, and to persist in face of casualties, just as they do with military means. The entire population—men, women, children, youth, adults, and the elderly—and all institutions of the society can participate in the struggle. They will, therefore, all need the opportunity to improve their capacity to wage this type of defense of their society. Preparedness and understanding will contribute to confidence and readiness to join the defense as the situation and policy may require. In crises, the society's regular institutions would become defense organizations, geared to resist control by the attackers and to defeat their objectives. The institutions should be able to retain democratic self-direction when under attack, and thereby make the society unrulable by foreign invaders or internal usurpers. This situation differs fundamentally from the confusion, bewilderment, and feelings of helplessness which have often occurred immediately following a coup d'état or an invasion.

The greater the solidarity of the population against the attack, the greater the chances of success. Historical experience with improvised nonviolent struggle, as in Denmark and Norway during the Nazi occupations, shows that such resistance can be effective, even in the presence of some collaboration with the attackers. Efforts will be needed, however, to minimize and control collaboration.

In the face of attack, the defenders need to begin their struggle immediately. The special strategies for the initial period are "nonviolent 'Blitzkrieg'"[3] and "communication and warning" to the attacker. These differ, but share two objectives: (1) to communicate to all concerned that the attack will be met by determined resistance by particularly insidious means; and (2) to accustom the population to active participation in the defense struggle from the start.

Either of these strategies can be applied singly in the initial period; both may be applied simultaneously; or either one may follow the other before the defense struggle shifts to more long-term strategies.

The strategy of communication and warning aims only to achieve the above two objectives. It may therefore, appear to be quite mild to the uninitiated. That is a deceptive impression, however. This strategy is mild only as the cocking and aiming of a pistol are mild in relation to the subsequent firing.

The strategy of nonviolent 'Blitzkrieg'—quick, sharp, full paralysis of the system—is a dramatic massive demonstration of resistance and defiance. Besides the two objectives cited above, it may also— the chances are not great—induce a quick retreat or capitulation by the attackers by giving them a bitter taste of future problems. Let us look at both of these strategies in more detail.

THE DEFENDERS' FIRST STRATEGIES:
(1) NONVIOLENT 'BLITZKRIEG'

The nonviolent 'Blitzkrieg' is a major thrust of defiance and near-total noncooperation, an attempt to defeat the attack by a lightning-quick campaign. This strategy would most likely be used when the attackers are perceived to be relatively weak and uncertain in their decision to attack, while the defending society feels itself to be strong, with a well-prepared and powerful defense policy. Such attackers are much more likely to be intimidated and bewildered by the paralysis than powerful attackers with strong determination. The latter may simply respond to the frontal attack by massive repression, which might be minimized by using instead a different strategy.

The strategy of nonviolent 'Blitzkrieg' may use the following weapons: a general strike, an economic shutdown, evacuation of cities, stay-at-home, paralysis of the political system, persistent operation of "business as usual" by government employees (ignoring the attackers' demands), filling the streets with demonstrators (or leaving them completely empty), massive attempts to subvert the attackers' troops and functionaries, and defiant publication of newspapers and radio broadcasts with news of the attack and resistance. There are many other possibilities.

Such massive defiance is intended to communicate to the attackers' leadership two things: (1) the civilian defenders are capable of a longer struggle which can deny the attackers the fruits of victory; and (2) the long-term effects of the defenders' actions and influence on the morale, loyalty, and obedience of the attackers' troops and functionaries may be politically fatal. Even if the defenders' goal of a quick victory is not achieved, at the very least such action will clearly communicate the intent to defend against the attack and the particular nature of the defense. The massive defiance will also warn of future difficulties if the attackers do not withdraw. When this nonviolent 'Blitzkrieg' is employed, a sharp distinction does not exist between the initial stage of communication and warning and the serious substantive defense struggle.

Only a very remarkable initial defiance by the civilian defenders and a most unusual leadership of the attacking forces (capable of recognizing unpleasant facts and of admitting an error and reversing directions) will make possible a quick end of the struggle with success to the defenders.

The nonviolent character of this strong strategy is more likely, however, to induce a calculated retreat from the attack than is an attempted military defense. In the latter case, the dynamics of military conflict and the loss of life operate strongly to prevent an early halt to a war in which there is as yet no military decision. Cancellation of the attack would appear to be surrender when there are lives to be avenged. The international complications of a military attack in Europe, and the probable rapidity of their development, work against a quick end to a military conflict there. This is especially the case because the conflict would be one between Communist and non-Communist states in which the issues at stake are major and the military capacities vast.

An early end to a conflict in which the defenders are fighting by civilian-based defense is a serious possibility, however. In this case, the dynamics of a military conflict are absent, while efforts can be made to maintain communication between the attackers and defenders during the conflict. Third-party pressures for a withdrawal or for mediation are also much more likely to be successful. A variety of face-saving formulae could be developed to ease the attackers' humiliation. (For example, it could be claimed that intelligence reports of hostile foreign military bases in the attacked country had proved false; that the new policy had been wrongly perceived as a guise hiding aggressive military intentions; that now-departed military commanders or government officials had launched the attack without authorization; or even that the operation had been successful and was now completed.)

If the initial nonviolent 'Blitzkrieg' strategy is not successful, the defenders will nevertheless have mobilized their forces, communicated their intent to resist, and indicated the special character of their defense. They will then need to shift strategy to another more suited to the longer-term struggle which is aimed to deny the attackers' specific objectives.

THE DEFENDERS' FIRST STRATEGIES:
(2) COMMUNICATION AND WARNING

In cases in which a nonviolent 'Blitzkrieg' strategy is not initially attempted, the strategy of "communication and warning" can be applied. By words and actions, the civilian defenders will seek to convey the message that a vigorous and powerful civilian-based defense struggle will be waged, a type especially difficult to counteract and defeat.

A variety of means can be applied to convey this message, including leaflets, letters, radio and television broadcasts, personal conversations, newspapers, posters, banners, use of diplomatic channels, United Nations meetings, third-party assistance, messages and slogans painted on walls, and special types of demonstrations in the attacked country which may communicate despite linguistic barriers. Personal conversations, painted wall messages, special types of demonstration, and leaflets were used in Czechoslovakia to communicate with Soviet troops in August 1968.[4] All these possibilities can be refined and prepared. Advance study of the languages and cultures of potential attackers can help such communication.

Some of these efforts will be aimed at the leaders of the attacking regime or group, who may not have recognized the will and capacity of the attacked society for powerful defense. A small chance may still exist to induce them to halt the attack if their perception of reality can be corrected.

Some of the communication and warning will also be aimed directly and indirectly at the attackers' general population and potential supporters—in their home country in the case of invasion, or within one's own society in the case of a coup d'état. It may be necessary to correct lies the home population has been told about the attack, and it is important to help them to dissent and to oppose the attack. The nonviolent character of the defense will make such opposition to the attack less difficult than would military defense, in which relatives and friends in the military forces are being killed, and opponents of the war are often viewed as traitors.

In contrast, in the absence of violent resistance, appeals for noncooperation and disobedience by the attackers' troops may be effective. The radio broadcast appeals of President Charles de Gaulle and Prime Minister M. Debré to the French people at the time of the

1961 generals' 'Putsch' in Algiers were beamed to conscript soldiers in Algeria, many of whom had transistor radios. Those appeals were crucial in the refusal of the conscripts to support their officers' coup.[5]

Words and actions to communicate the intent to defend and the means by which the defense will be conducted will also be aimed at one's neighboring countries, at one's allies (in cases of civilian-based defense treaty organizations), and at the general international community. This communication will lay the groundwork for assistance, for avoidance of action which would harm the defense, and for international diplomatic, moral, economic, and political pressures against the attack.

Descriptions of the defense to be offered will also be important for one's own population, particularly for any possible sections of it which may have been only minimally involved in preparations and training or inadequately informed about the defense policy. (In a well-prepared country, that condition should not, of course, exist.) The population will hear at this point the message that their preparations will now bear fruit, that their whole society is becoming involved in a highly important defense struggle, and that they have an important role to play in it. This will support specific preparations and actions in their neighborhoods and work places, and contribute to the growth of the general spirit of resistance in the population as a whole.

Domestic sympathizers of the attackers and persons who may opportunistically seek to enrich themselves or to gain a position of power will also need to be warned during this period. By words and actions they will be told that the defense will be strong and waged by the whole society. They will be informed that, because of the type of resistance, no physical harm will be done to them. However, if they collaborate, they too will become targets of persistent resistance. They will be regarded as betrayers of their own people and prevented from retaining any rewards from the attackers.

The individual troops and functionaries of the attacking forces will be especially important targets for influence during this stage of the struggle. One of the key ways to dissolve the occupation or coup is to weaken and remove the loyalty, reliability, and obedience of the attackers' troops and functionaries. They may have been deceived about the situation, what to expect from the population, or even what country they have invaded!

The civilian defenders will strive to communicate the following: the issues at stake in the conflict as the defenders perceive them; the principles and practices of the society which has been attacked; the perceived goals of the attackers; and the importance for the peoples of both countries or groups that the attack be abandoned.

The defenders will also seek to inform the troops and functionaries that the resisting population will aim to defeat the attack and defend the society without threatening the lives and personal safety of the individuals in the attacking forces.

Such contacts and information will lay the basis for later appeals to be deliberately mild or inefficient in applying repression, to aid the population and resisters in specific ways, to ignore orders for harsh actions, to mutiny openly, or to "disappear" into the countryside or among the defending population, which will help them. In such ways the attackers' capacity for repression and administration may be, under certain conditions, slowly or rapidly dissolved.

A variety of the means of communication by words and action listed at the beginning of this section will be used to reach all these groups. In addition, drawn or painted symbols, significant colors, flags at half mast, tolling of bells, silence, wailing of sirens, certain songs, and many variations on these may be used to convey opposition to the attack and determination to resist.

Direct symbolic intervention and obstruction may also be used. For example, persons may block with their bodies bridges, highways, streets, entrances to towns, cities, and buildings. They may block highways, railway stations, and airports with abandoned automobiles or dismantled machinery to make the facilities inoperative. In advance of the entry of attacking troops (so that there is no risk of loss of life) certain demolitions—as of bridges—and other destruction of one's own property may be beneficial. (This must not be done at a later stage, however, in order to prevent sliding into a self-destructive strategy of sabotage and guerrilla warfare.[6]) Parts could be removed from key machinery at any point, and any records and computerized data which might be useful to the attackers could be destroyed.

Most of these types of action rely primarily for their impact on psychological or moral influences. Although mechanical obstructions may physically impede or delay the dispersion of troops or the occupation of certain locations or facilities, even they have mainly a psychological impact, because in time they can be overcome. The loss of bridges may delay the advance of invading troops, but will not prevent it. The destruction of information on one's own society and population is, however, likely to be a serious impediment to certain goals of attackers, especially those requiring economic data, information on individuals, locating of resisters, and establishment of a new subservient government.

Another category of actions may also be used initially: brief applications of such methods of noncooperation as the general strike, economic shut-down, massive stay-at-home, or closing of all government offices, for example. Nonviolent 'Blitzkrieg' and sustained defense struggle employ some of these same methods, but in lengthier applications. These brief actions not only communicate opposition and intent to resist. They also impart an understanding of the more persistent and substantial means of defense which the attackers will face if they do not call a halt. The weapons used in the defense will progressively shift from largely symbolic ones to the more directly power-wielding forms of noncooperation.

Dramatic forms of intervention may also be used at this stage. These may include: massive defiance of curfews, persistent conduct of "business as usual" both economically and politically (on the basis of the legitimate laws and practices), holding of street parties for all (including the hostile troops), and large-scale efforts to induce disaffection and undermine the loyalty of the troops and minor functionaries. These various methods of symbolic action, noncooperation, or intervention may be used singly or in sequences and combinations deemed appropriate to the particular situation.

The attackers' countermeasures to these initial forms of communication and warning by words and actions are difficult to predict. They may range from extremely mild to very brutal, even in the same situation.

It is possible that the attackers may at this stage call off the venture, saving face as best they can, but such withdrawal is unlikely. The resisters must be prepared to carry on the defense on the assumption that the struggle will be extended and difficult. Whether the initial defense strategy has been a nonviolent 'Blitzkrieg', a campaign of communication and warning, or both (in sequence or in combination), a decision will at some point have to be made on how to carry on a more sustained and powerful defense struggle.

SHIFTING STRATEGIES FOR
SUSTAINED STRUGGLE

In military wars the defenders may want, and attempt to achieve, a quick, decisive victory, but no demoralization or sense of defeat need follow their failure to do so. A shift of strategy for the next stage of the struggle may then be required. In civilian wars of defense this is also true. A shift of strategy to one suitable for the next phase is therefore no reason for demoralization, but rather the opposite. The shift is a demonstration that the defenders are taking the initiative in shaping the struggle to help bring eventual victory.

No single blueprint can be created to plan civilian-based defense for all countries, situations, and contingencies. Nor can a single resistance method, such as the general strike, be used effectively everywhere. That is much more true of civilian means than of military means.

The strategies, tactics, and methods of civilian-based defense provide great flexibility to confront and defeat the attackers' objectives. In civilian-based defense the political, social, economic, and psychological weaponry applied in any given case can be directly related to the specific issue at stake, the attackers' objectives, and the selected defense strategies.

It is highly advantageous to study in advance all types of possible attacks and potential enemy objectives extremely carefully in order to develop civilian resistance plans to defeat them. Such plans would include the selection of the specific weapons (psychological, social, economic, or political) most appropriate for defeating those objectives. This differs from conventional military and nuclear means in which—while strategy and tactics may be complex and highly variable—the weapons are those which simply destroy and kill. This is true even though the issues at stake in the particular conflict are unlikely to be destruction and killing as such, but instead economic, political, ideological, territorial, or whatever. With civilian-based defense, the defenders require particular types of methods which can block directly achievement of the attackers' objectives. (Additional types of methods may, of course, also be needed for other aspects of the conflict.)

The choice of strategies, tactics, and methods for use in a particular conflict will be influenced by diverse factors. The nature and relative importance of the issues at stake for the attacking and defending groups and the type of attack which has been launched are important among these. Other factors are the nature of the attacking group or regime, its vulnerabilities, the intensity of means of action and repression it uses, and the feelings of closeness or distance between the conflicting parties. The degree to which the attackers are subject to influence or pressures from third parties, and the degree to which third parties can be influenced by the defenders must also be considered.[7]

A final major factor influencing the choice of how to wage civilian-based defense is the internal strength of the attacked society.[8] This includes the status of its independent institutions, the adequacy of preparations and training for this policy, the society's vulnerability or self-reliance economically, the willingness of the defenders to sustain casualties as the price of defense, and the degree of domestic collaboration or support the attacker may encounter or be able to elicit.

Many specific methods of struggle were used in the improvised cases listed in Table One in Chapter 2. Many additional ones have also been used on a variety of issues in other cases.[9] Certain of these are listed in Table Three. These methods and others would be available for use in prepared civilian-based defense.

The variations and complexities in Western European societies and in their experience using these methods should contribute to flexibility and resourcefulness in the choice, modification, and application of these nonviolent weapons. This flexibility is necessary, since the defense needs of Western European countries will differ, depending on whether the attack is a coup d'état or an invasion and also on the objectives of the attack.

The civilian defenders will also need to consider by which of the three recognized mechanisms of change in nonviolent struggle — conversion, accommodation, or nonviolent coercion—they prefer to achieve victory.[10] They may wish to convert the attackers to the view that the objectives of the attack and the attack itself are unjustified. They may be willing to accommodate, as is done in most strikes: each side gives way to some degree and receives a portion of its original objectives. The defenders may, however, aim nonviolently to coerce the attackers into abandoning both their original goals and the attack itself.

Table Three. Some Available Defense Weapons.

---

symbolic protests
paralysis of transportation
social boycotts
specific and general strikes
civil disobedience
economic shutdowns
political noncooperation
"disappearance" under false identities
economic boycotts
public demonstrations
slow-downs
publication of banned newspapers
deliberate inefficiencies in carrying out orders
assistance to persecuted people
broadcasts about resistance on radio and television
public defiance by the legislature
judicial resistance
defiance by the government executive
denial of legitimacy to the usurpers
noncooperation by civil servants
legislative procrastinations and delays
declarations of defiance
persistent continuation of old policies and laws
student defiance
children's demonstrations
individual and mass resignations
refusal of collaboration
maintenance of autonomy of independent organizations and institutions
subversion of the usurpers' troops, and incitement of them to mutiny

---

In special cases—as when the foreign attackers' home regime is in a precarious condition, or when the attacker is an internal usurper—a fourth mechanism of change may be sought. The defenders may seek not simply to coerce the attacking group or regime but to bring about its disintegration, so that it no longer even exists as a political unit able to capitulate.

In practice, the mechanisms of conversion, accommodation, and nonviolent coercion are often intimately blended. A preference for one or the other will, however, strongly affect the choice of the grand strategy for the defense and also of the particular methods of action applied.

In the case of a coup d'état, the aim of the defenders would usually be to disintegrate the usurping group as an effective political unit, since the other options would allow it to become a future threat. Also, bargaining with it could be viewed as recognizing its right to lay claim to control of the state apparatus.

In the case of invasions, disintegration of the invaders' government in their own country can occur only in very special circumstances, all of which are beyond the direct control of the civilian defenders in the attacked country. Disintegration of the attackers' home government must therefore normally be kept as a remote possibility, and the choice of strategies, tactics, and methods for the defenders be based on considerations of the mechanisms of conversion, accommodation, and nonviolent coercion operating within the defending country.

The most likely, and usually preferred, process will be a combination of all three mechanisms. Conversion would be largely limited to occupation troops and some officials (under most conditions), while mixtures of accommodation and coercion would operate on the regime which had launched the attack. The occupation forces may finally collapse in a morass of indiscipline and chaos, or they may withdraw because their leaders recognize victory to be impossible. The top officials may regret only their failure, not the choice of their original goal nor the attack itself. Clearly, the capacity to wield power is of primary importance in conducting successful civilian-based defense. That must be remembered in waging the defense struggle.

6 DEFEATING ATTACK

DEFEATING OCCUPATIONS

Civilian-based defense does not require more courage or greater heroism than conventional military defense. It does, however, require more of both than does the present nuclear strategy, which is based on a preference for risking nuclear disaster rather than for mobilizing courage and capacity to defeat a threatened Soviet occupation. Courage alone, however, is insufficient. It must be combined with wisdom and shrewdness in the selection of strategies and tactics, and persistence and discipline in their application.

When it is clear that the defenders' first strategies of nonviolent 'Blitzkrieg' and of communication and warning have served their purposes, but have been insufficient to force the invaders to withdraw, a shift to long-term strategies is required. These are designed to achieve the aims discussed previously: retain the maximum possible self-control by the defending society, prevent the attackers from establishing effective political control of the invaded country, deny the attackers their objectives, and inflict grave political, economic, morale, diplomatic, and other losses.

In facing the strategic problems of substantive defense, the civilian defenders can either mount a massive campaign of total noncooperation and defiance (similar to an extended nonviolent 'Blitzkrieg', discussed in Chapter 5) or initiate various forms of selective resistance. The defenders may also use each of these major strategies at different times to meet special needs of the defense.

Massive, total resistance—consisting of campaigns of comprehensive noncooperation and defiance by the entire society against the attackers' regime and its policies as a whole—may be appropriate at certain stages of the substantive defense. These would involve significantly greater strategic noncooperation than has occurred in past improvised cases of nonviolent struggle against occupation regimes. If used, this strategy is likely to be applied temporarily to achieve particular purposes, such as to halt brutalities, force abandonment of conscript labor, or secure food supplies. The total resistance strategy may also be applied towards the end of a longer selective resistance struggle. The strategy might then be applied to secure final defeat of the attackers when they are believed to be already seriously weakened. The aim of total resistance at this point is to strike a knock-out blow to defeat or disintegrate the attackers' regime or controls, to destroy their ability to continue the whole venture, and to restore the society's independence and freedom.

The defenders should carefully choose the points in the struggle at which total noncooperation may be effectively used. This strategy is not suitable for extended use, and should not be thoughtlessly applied as an emotional response to the original attack or to an especially horrific act by the attackers' forces.

Even if the attackers' repression is not extreme or can be withstood without unbearable suffering, total resistance imposes major costs on the defenders by shutting down necessary aspects of their own society. It is extremely difficult to apply except for special situations and limited periods. The defending population must be able to survive the defense struggles. Extended application would require an exceptionally strong, well-prepared, and self-reliant society. Various European societies have great resilience, but at present none is sufficiently self-reliant and prepared for civilian-based defense to apply total noncooperation for extended periods. These societies could take steps to increase their capacity to apply total noncooperation.

Total resistance may not be used at all in certain civilian-based defense struggles because of its special characteristics and requirements. In some cases, within a grand strategy of selective resistance, total noncooperation may be used at specific points to achieve particular objectives. A few examples will illustrate this. Total resistance may be applied when a specific objectionable policy or aim has already been seriously weakened, or when its implementation has been blocked in order to force the attackers to abandon the policy or objective completely. For example, where special campaigns have forced the attackers to retreat from efforts to introduce fascist or Communist ideology into the schools, a brief total noncooperation campaign could be started to force the attackers formally to abandon all claims and efforts to control education.

In a very different situation, total noncooperation might be used to demonstrate defiance and determination after the opponents' troops or police have inflicted severe brutalities. More extended use of the total resistance strategy should be restricted to the times in which the attackers' capacity to exercise control has been significantly weakened—when their troops are on the verge of mutiny, for example—or when some other potentially decisive condition exists. In those cases the defenders must be able to sustain total noncooperation for a long period despite possible severe repression.

With those exceptions, the main thrust of the society's defense instead must be the strategy of selective resistance. When other strategies have been used (such as the nonviolent 'Blitzkrieg,' the strategy of communication and warning, and specific campaigns of total resistance), a shift of strategy will be required to the longer-term ways of struggle by selective resistance.

The strategy of selective resistance does not pretend to be total, but deliberately concentrates resistance on particular points or objectives which are especially important for the defense effort. This strategy has several advantages. For example, it enables the defense to be concentrated on those crucial objectives, instead of being diffused on a great variety of objectives and issues. This strategy is also less exhausting to the defending population, since in most cases the major responsibility to wage defense will shift from one section of the population to another as the specific points and issues of resistance change.

In choosing the points for selective resistance, the defenders will need to consider six major questions:

1. What are the attackers' main objectives?
2. What will prevent the attackers from gaining or maintaining control over the state apparatus or significant parts of it?

3. What will prevent the attackers from weakening or destroying the society's independent institutions and their capacity for resistance?
4. What are the specific issues which typify the general principles and objectives of the struggle?
5. What will enable the defenders to act in ways in which they can use their strongest issues, resources, and sections of the population (and avoid relying upon their weakest ones) to advance the defense?
6. What will concentrate defense strength on the especially vulnerable points in the attackers' system, regime, or policies, which if broken, will imperil the attackers' ability to achieve their objectives and to continue the occupation or attempt to rule?

Let us now look at why these questions are important for successful defense of Western European countries and how they might be answered.

1. What are the attackers' main objectives?

Denial of the attackers' main objectives is obviously crucial, and the defense must focus on means to achieve that. For example, if the Soviet Union attacked in order to impose on the country a Communist government, then establishment of such a government and consolidation of its control must be prevented. This would be accomplished by refusal to collaborate at all levels, isolation of any would-be collaborators, and denial to collaborators and invaders of control of the various government departments, police, prison system, and military forces. The defenders must also deny legitimacy to any new regime, massively refuse obedience to it and cooperation with it, and persist in maintaining loyalty to the principles and practices of their own system. The defense would thus be primarily political: strikes and boycotts on economic issues would not be appropriate.

If the foreign attack had been launched to gain economic objectives, then those objectives should be denied. This can be achieved by such means as refusal of cooperation and assistance by every person and institution involved (including workers, technicians, administrators, and scientists). This refusal would be applied at all relevant stages, such as procuring of raw materials, research, planning, transportation, manufacture, supply of energy and parts, quality control, and preparation for shipping. Interference and obstruction would also be possible at various stages.

If the Soviet Union launched the attack in order to spread its ideology, then resistance to efforts to denigrate the beliefs of one's own society and blocking of attempts to indoctrinate the population with the attackers' political beliefs would be crucial. These goals can be achieved by many kinds of noncooperation by persons and institutions involved in education, religion, newspapers and magazines, publishing, radio and television, youth activities, and government. Those persons and institutions would also press the virtues of the freedom of ideas. They would promote the variety of beliefs and philosophies of the attacked society, and praise the right of people to choose freely. At the same time, the defenders would attack both the intruders' doctrines and the concept that everyone ought to believe the same—especially the attackers' efforts to force them to do so.

Territorial and genocidal objectives are far more complex than the above cases and require separate analysis, at much greater length than is possible here, but some introductory insights can be suggested.

Territorial objectives could include seizure of small enclaves (as for a submarine base, an airfield, or small area producing important minerals or fuels) from which the indigenous population would usually be expelled, while the larger part of the country remained unoccupied and the population's life undisturbed.

Attackers might attempt seizure of large territories from which the indigenous population is to be removed and resettled, and the occupied area repopulated by people brought in by the attackers.

Finally, the attackers might aim to seize large territories in which the indigenous population would remain. The attackers might initiate only limited immigration of other people. The invaders may in such cases be indifferent to the indigenous people, or they may wish to exploit them economically, or to incorporate them politically.

Since, as thus far conceived, civilian-based defense relies primarily on the resistance of the population and the society's institutions, a possible objective of attackers of seizing only small enclaves appears to be the most difficult to resist by this policy. Conversely, the aim of seizing and operating a populated society appears to be the least difficult to resist successfully. However, the problem of defeating efforts to seize small enclaves by civilian-based defense has not yet been seriously examined. Any dependence of the attackers in the enclave on the surrounding territory for water, fuel, food, or labor would provide points of leverage which might be used for resistance. Whether they would be effective, or to what degree, would depend on the extent of the dependence, the risks which the population in the unoccupied territory was willing to take, and the difficulties and cost to the invaders of importing those necessities from elsewhere.

Rather than thinking of classic self-reliant civilian-based defense strategies for this situation, it might be more useful to explore other ways to pressure the invaders. This could be done, for example, with support from sympathetic third countries, or with United Nations political and economic pressures. Organized action by dock workers, pilots, airport workers, and others throughout the world could halt travel, transportation, and shipping of needed materials. In very special situations only, nonviolent invasions might be launched into the enclave, as Indian volunteers marched into the Portuguese enclave of Goa in May and June 1955. Smaller applications of the same method were also applied in other Portuguese enclaves in India. Another option might be to use radio broadcasts, smuggled literature, airlifted leaflets, and other means to distribute to the attackers' home population, functionaries, and troops information on how to use nonviolent struggle against their own government.

More generally, however, the attacked country as a whole might apply various types of noncooperation to the invaders' control of the enclave or to the attackers' home country—border closings, economic sanctions, denial of labor, international protests, and diplomatic actions—as suggested by Spanish measures against British control of Gibraltar and Cuban measures against United States' control of the naval base at Guantanamo Bay. The latter situations also suggest that military action in such cases has often been judged to be neither a simple and effective response nor a desirable one, even by governments with an army. Work is needed on this problem.

The attackers' objective of seizing territory with expulsion and resettlement of the population offers significantly more points of contact between the attackers' forces and the population. Opportunities exist for noncooperation to delay or block deportation measures, for action to undermine the reliability and efficiency of the troops, officials, and others assigned to effect the population transfers, and for efforts to arouse the support of third parties on which the attackers are economically or politically dependent. Maintaining nonviolent discipline in the resistance would be important in these cases. It would help prevent the attackers from shifting to genocidal actions or to other mass attacks on the population (as poisoning, gassing, neutron bombing, and the like), which would more likely occur during wartime conditions.

Massive expulsion and resettlement without the cooperation of the displaced population is an exceptionally difficult task, requiring vast allocation of personnel, transportation, and economic resources. It also requires considerable time, during which policy and personnel shifts in the attackers' home government could take place. Even if expulsion is successful, the struggle would not be over. Movements could then begin for reestablishment of a homeland for the displaced people, or their descendants, as the struggles of Jews to establish and develop a homeland, and of the Palestinians to do similarly, illustrate. There are grounds to believe that nonviolent action can provide options those groups have not fully considered. Here, too, specialized attention is needed.

The attackers' objective of seizing large territories with their indigenous population most clearly requires the submission and cooperation of the population. These can be refused by the various strategies and methods of civilian-based defense discussed above and below. In addition to the use of outright noncooperation by the indigenous population, the resisters would aim once more to influence the occupiers' troops and functionaries, home population, and the international community to secure pressures against the occupation and annexation. There is a long European history of nations whose territory has been annexed by others which have survived as a people and culture to regain independence in later years, decades, and even centuries. Ireland, Poland, and the European nations ruled by the Ottoman Empire are examples in Europe. Most of the rest of the world consists of countries which have liberated themselves from one European empire or another. Because of the extensive advance preparations and training, the process of liberation by prepared civilian-based defense should take place significantly faster than it did in those examples of cultural and national survival.

Genocidal objectives are far more difficult to combat than the other objectives of attackers but, contrary to popular impressions, their defeat is sometimes possible. That is apparently more possible by noncooperation than by violent means, which in certain cases appear to have facilitated genocide. It is now clear that both Hitler and Goebbels concluded that the outbreak of war in Europe made politically possible the actual extermination program against Jews, Gypsies, and others, which was adopted in stages between March 1941 and summer 1942. War had broken out in early September 1939. Before the war and well into it, regardless of Hitler's ultimate aim, the actual policy was not extermination but induced emigration. Gerald Reitlinger, a scholar of the Holocaust, reports that as late as August and September 1939, "It does not seem that at this period systematic extermination of the Jews was considered."[1] (This differs from murders and particular massacres which did happen.) Mass systematic killings of Jews began in December 1941, after the United States entered the war. The Gross-Wansee Conference at which the German bureaucracy was directed to the task of genocide was held on 20 January 1942, and the following month the term "Final Solution" was being used in official rulings.[2]

Once the Holocaust was under way, the war did not save the Jews. "Fortunately," Goebbels wrote in his diary, "a whole series of possibilities presents itself for us in wartime that would be denied us in peacetime."[3] Between four-and-one-half and six million Jews were exterminated as well as many Gypsies, Eastern Europeans, and others. The end of the war and Himmler's anticipation of defeat did, however, prevent the deaths of many more.

We must recognize fully the horror and disaster that was inflicted on the Jewish people in particular. It is also important to recognize that during the main thrust of the extermination program, the Nazis did not succeed in killing nearly as many Jews as they wanted. The percentages saved deserve notice. They vary from relatively small portions in some countries to over 80 percent of all Jews in France, over 90 percent in Fascist Italy, all Belgian Jews (and half of the foreign Jews there), almost all of the Danish Jews, and all Bulgarian Jews who were citizens.[4] During the Holocaust itself they were saved, when it happened, not by the war or violent resistance, but by the noncooperation of people whose help was needed to carry out the extermination program. These included, variously, the intended victims themselves, the general populations of the occupied countries, the governments of those countries, and non-Nazi German officials, military personnel, and civil servants. Some people in all of these groups refused at various points to cooperate.[5] That is what appears to have saved so many. We desperately require major research to give us additional information and understanding. The "lesson" all too many have learned from the Holocaust—that Jews were doomed because of too little violent opposition to the Nazis and were saved by the war—is a false one. It seems from this case that the war provided the necessary precondition for the extermination and that nonviolent noncooperation was responsible for saving millions of Jews.

With advance preparations and training based on major work on how to prevent and defeat future attempts at genocide, civilian-based defense might be capable of defeating even foreign invaders intent on genocide. These means of struggle then need to be compared to their military counterparts, including the risk of annihilation in a nuclear Holocaust of the population being "defended."

2. What will prevent the attackers from gaining or maintaining control over the state apparatus or significant parts of it?

Even if the invaders' main objective is not to impose a government of their own liking, much less to restructure the political system on their own model, selective resistance is necessary to defend the country's political system. This is because the attackers require time to achieve almost any objective they may have. This means they must either secure the submissive assistance of the existing government and its agencies, or they must impose a new government to carry out their objectives and to control the population.

It is therefore crucial that the defenders prevent submission and collaboration by the existing government, including the system of administration, institutions of control, police, military, and any other divisions which might serve the attackers to help gain their objectives or establish control over the society. It is also crucial that the defenders prevent the establishment and consolidation of a substitute regime to serve the attackers' goals.

The methods of resistance described above to defeat the attackers' main objectives are generally also suitable to block the attackers from gaining control of the state apparatus, as to impose a Communist or other government, for example. Specifically, the following forms of resistance are available: legislative, executive, and judicial defiance and obstruction; persistent application by civil servants and bureaucrats of the previously established policies, laws, and constitutional principles; strikes by those same government employees; refusal by police and any remaining military personnel and units to cooperate or to carry out orders of an illegal regime; denial of legitimacy to any collaborationist or usurping regime by the general population; massive refusal by the population to obey and cooperate with a collaborationist or usurping regime; and the assertive maintenance or establishment of alternative means (outside any newly established illegal regime) to meet the society's needs and to maintain order independently of the attackers' controls. If these methods are successfully used, failure to control and utilize the state apparatus will imperil the attackers' achievement of their other objectives.

3. What will prevent the attackers from weakening or destroying the society's independent institutions and their capacity for resistance?

Preservation of the autonomy and capacity for action of the society's independent institutions is important in a civilian-based defense struggle for two reasons. First, such institutions are required to provide the structural basis for organized nonviolent struggle. Second, the attackers may deliberately seek to subordinate or destroy those institutions in order to give themselves a free hand in restructuring the political system.

While at times the actions of individuals and the spontaneous mobilization of unorganized people can have major political influence, the impact of resistance is infinitely greater when people act through organizations and institutions. This is true of such groups as families, religious institutions, trade unions, management groups, cultural organizations, educational associations and institutions, political parties, various voluntary organizations, neighborhood groupings, villages, towns, cities, provinces, and smaller governmental bodies. Actions by them to defy and to refuse to cooperate with invaders can wield considerable power and help to defeat the attackers. That is why Solidarity as a mass organized institution, even when under repression, has been able to wield so much more power in Poland than did the same number of isolated and unorganized individual workers in earlier years. Norwegian resistance during the Nazi occupation is an excellent example of the way independent institutions, such as the schools and the churches, can defend their society.[6]

Selective resistance may be required to defend the society's independent institutions. The attackers may intend to establish total control, eliminate the possibility of effective resistance to their new order, or restructure the whole society on a totalitarian model.[7] They may therefore attempt to abolish the autonomy of all existing independent institutions, maintain them only in emasculated submissive forms, or destroy them outright. In their place, the attackers may create centrally controlled institutions consistent with a totalitarian model, to facilitate control of their members. All such efforts by the attackers become necessary points for selective resistance if the society is to be able to resist future controls and to dissolve the new oppressive regime. For example, the earlier resistance of the Catholic Church in Poland resulted in its survival as a strong independent institution outside the full control of the Communist Party and the state. This independence was later very important in the development of Solidarity and related organizations aiming to democratize Poland.[8]

4. What are the specific issues which typify the general principles and objectives of the struggle?

Civilian defenders can advance their cause by weakening the attackers' will and power to gain their goals and by strengthening their own will and power to block those goals. Skillful sharpening of the issue is important in doing this. The civilian defenders can sharpen such broad issues as "independence" and "freedom" by locating specific applications which epitomize in concentrated form the defenders' aims and their conflicts with the invaders' contrasting objectives. For example, a ban against public assemblies will appear most unjustified and in conflict with the principles of the defending society if the resistance focuses on the defiant holding of religious services, instead of, say, rallies to keep the bars open, or even demonstrations to protest the ban itself. Repression and brutalities against those attending or leading the religious services will in turn seem especially outrageous, and be more likely to shift opinion and support away from the attackers and to the defenders.

Use of such a narrower focus is not a matter of being moderate in one's aims, but of concentrating one's strength in ways which will make victory more likely. The defenders choose as the point of concentrated defense a specific expression of the general problem which symbolizes it in extreme form and is least defensible by the opponent. That point is simultaneously most capable of arousing the greatest resistance strength against it. Success on such specific points increases the defenders' self-confidence and ability to gain their wider objectives.

Future civilian-based defense struggles in Western Europe might therefore concentrate resistance on defense of specific aspects of the society's way of life. These might include freedom of religion and speech, continuation of democratic institutions, free labor, educational freedom, children's and parents' rights, care of the ill and injured, social services, food, water, fuel, use of one's language, and respect for national symbols. Concentrated focus on such issues was a considerable help in various past struggles, including that in Norway during the Nazi occupation and that in Poland in the establishment and development of Solidarity. These specific aspects would help mobilize the maximum determination and solidarity for defense, while making the invaders' position more vulnerable and weak.

5. What will enable the defenders to act in ways in which they can use their strongest issues, resources, and sections of the population (and avoid relying upon their weakest ones) to advance the defense?

Unless the defending society is sufficiently prepared, self-reliant, and strong to apply the strategy of total noncooperation, it will do well to concentrate its available force. This is done partly by selecting strategies determined by consideration of the above four major questions. Another key factor is the relative strength and weakness of the various population groups and institutions of the society as defense forces. For example, if trade unions are very strong and church groups very weak, it would be better (other factors being equal) to rely on the unions instead of the churches to carry out major parts of the defense struggle. In general, it is necessary to assess the relative internal strength and capacity for defense resistance of various occupational, professional, cultural, political, and other groups. The stronger should normally be relied upon to play major roles in the resistance, while efforts are made to strengthen and defend the weaker ones. There may be particular circumstances which require that action be taken despite weaknesses, but even then consideration of one's real strength is required.

6. What will concentrate defense strength on the especially vulnerable points in the attackers' system, regime, or policies, which, if broken, will imperil their ability to achieve their objectives and to continue the occupation or attempt to rule?

A first step is to identify the supports of the attackers' system and specifically of their aggression. These may include, for example, major international economic dependencies, as in currency support, food, essential supplies, markets, or energy. The supports may also include the regime's legitimacy, bestowed by powerful religious groups. Perhaps the government or system requires the continuing support of persons or groups which are not fully a part of the ruling group. Certainly, the necessary supports include the assistance of home government and occupation government agencies, bureaucracies, departments, police, and military forces.

Once the necessary supports have been identified, they must be weakened and removed. A second step, accordingly, is to plan and undertake deliberate measures, which may operate directly or indirectly, to undermine and collapse the supports needed to continue the occupation and repression in the invaded country. It is true that sometimes in improvised nonviolent struggles such supports have weakened or collapsed without conscious efforts by the resisters to undermine them. In other cases, the undermining has been deliberate. For example, students and others in Prague in August 1968 intentionally sought by conversations, leaflets, and other means to persuade Soviet troops that their invasion and occupation was unjustified.[9] Conscious efforts may be made to influence the views and actions of people and groups which may possibly restrict and withdraw their support fot the occupation or even oppose it actively.

Sometimes these efforts may operate indirectly, for example, when extreme violence is perpetrated against courageous nonviolent resisters. This may produce revulsion even among the attackers' usual supporters. This can lead to dissent, internal conflicts, withdrawal of support, and even mutiny among the attackers' normal backers, troops and functionaries. That is one reason why maintenance of nonviolent discipline is so important for the defenders.

Besides these indirect ways of undermining of support for the attackers, a major effort is also required to apply direct pressures to undermine the support of the identified groups, institutions, persons, and resources without which the attackers' regime and system will collapse. In civilian-based defense the prior studies, contingency plans, preparations, and training can multiply the ability to identify the necessary supports and to subject them to systematic undermining. This can disintegrate the attackers' capacity to continue the aggression and even to rule their own political system. Then the whole system may collapse, just as Samson's concentrated strength on the pillars caused the whole temple to fall.

By answering the above six questions, it becomes possible for the defenders to choose major points for selective resistance and to mobilize their defense struggles primarily around them. If they are chosen wisely, and if the defense is developed and applied skillfully, bravely, and persistently, an effective defense will be possible. The attackers' objectives can then be denied and their attempts to control the state apparatus defeated. The society's independent institutions can survive as vital agents for the operation, self-control, and defense of the society. The selection of the pivotal issues will help achieve the maximum mobilization of the defending society's population. It will undermine the attackers' "justification" for the aggression, and therefore of support for it, among their home population, supporters, and third parties. The defenders will become more able to utilize their strongest resources for their own defense, while undermining the attackers at their most vulnerable points. All this, done with intelligence, determination, and persistence in the face of casualties, undermines the attackers' ability to achieve their goals and even to continue their occupation. Victory for the civilian defenders comes into view.

DEFEATING COUPS D'ÉTAT

Coups d'état, it should be remembered, constitute a serious defense problem. Apart from civil war, civilian-based defense is the only available policy for dealing with this security threat. Several European countries have already used improvised noncooperation to defeat coups d'état. The clearest cases are Germany against the Kapp 'Putsch' in 1920, and France against the Algiers generals' 'Putsch' in 1961.[10] Noncooperation was the only means of defense used in the 1920 case and the main means used—despite talk of military action—in the 1961 case. In both instances, the noncooperation was government policy. The cases are very different, but both demonstrate that the legitimate government may be saved by action of ordinary people, civil servants, or loyal officers and regular soldiers, acting nonviolently to preserve it and to undermine the group attempting to seize power.

There have also been other relevant European cases. In August 1968 the Soviet Union clearly expected that, with its swift military occupation of Czechoslovakia and the seizure of top reform Party and government officials, it would be possible to stage a coup by trusted Stalinists. Popular resistance was too strong for that to happen, however. When the resistance radio reported rumors that certain Stalinists were about to form a substitute government, the social pressures were so powerful that those persons quickly issued denials. It proved necessary for the Russians to negotiate with the very officials they had kidnapped immediately following the invasion of August 21. The Russians then allowed them to resume their official positions which they held, keeping major parts of the reforms, until April of the following year—when Czechoslovak officials capitulated to new Russian pressures and Gustav Husak took over.[11]

In a more recent case, the declaration of martial law in Poland in December 1981 had the basic elements of a military coup d'état. The aim was not only to crush Solidarity but also to bypass regular Communist Party and governmental procedures. Consequently the resistance to the martial law regime of General Wojciech Jaruzelski is a relevant case of improvised resistance to coup d'état. That resistance continued over many months, but significantly did not, so far as is known, include major open defiance within the military forces or the governmental bureaucracy. In the German and French cases, however, there was major governmental opposition accompanied by lack of support or outright noncooperation within the military forces, and these coups were defeated within a few days.

In cases where the government has wide support, it is not a long way from these improvised cases to the launching of preparations and contingency planning to deter and defeat coups. The basic grand strategy of civilian-based defense for defeating coups d'état, executive usurpations, and other internal usurpations would aim to make impossible the consolidation of control of the state apparatus and the society by the usurpers. This would be done by denying authority to them and by the consequent disobedience and noncooperation by government employees, the general citizenry, and the society's institutions. Instead of submitting to the usurpers and assisting them, the employees, citizens, and institutions would insist on the return to constitutional principles and practices as the price of resuming their normal roles in the society, economy, and political system.

Quick, decisive victories against attempted internal usurpations appear to be most likely in cases in which seven key conditions are met. First, the society clearly repudiates the usurpers as illegitimate. Second, the general population actively opposes the coup and expresses that opposition through strong independent institutions. Third, the legitimate governmental leadership issues calls for resistance. Fourth, the government employees and governmental bodies, on various levels, denounce and refuse to cooperate with the usurpers. Fifth, the police do not support, and preferably denounce, the coup (refusing, for example, to arrest resisters on orders of the usurpers). Sixth, the military forces do not solidly back the coup, or they become disaffected (if they earlier backed it), and significant military sections, including regular troops, refuse to cooperate with it. (This applies whether the coup is launched by a section of the military or by a civilian group.) Lastly, as a result of these developments, the usurpers' power base and effectiveness crumble, while the legitimate government is widely supported and strengthened. The result is the collapse of the attempted seizure of power.

Diverse political groups which support a parliamentary system should see a common interest in preventing a military or political group from seizing control of the state apparatus and ousting them all in favor of an élite dictatorship. Indeed, it is quite possible that countries which have experienced or been threatened by coups— such as Spain, Greece, and Italy—might initiate civilian-based defense preparations for the limited purpose of preventing and defeating them. If coups d'état were recognized as serious security threats by NATO as a whole, the alliance could encourage such preparations and assist them by sharing feasibility studies, plans for suitable preparations, and training programs. Whether such steps were taken by individual countries on their own initiative or with alliance support, they would leave the regular military capacity and any alliance structure intact for dealing with international threats.

With increased understanding of the power capacity of prepared noncooperation and defiance, some countries might decide later to use that capacity also as one option in facing invasions and occupations. They might stop at that point, or move incrementally towards full transarmament. Other countries which introduced civilian-based defense to deter and defend against coups might keep the policy restricted to that single objective.

DEFYING REPRESSION

Whether directed against foreign occupation or internal usurpation, vigorous defense efforts will certainly not please the attackers. On the contrary, they are likely correctly to perceive the various civilian-based defense strategies as dangerous to their goals, venture, and system. At times, the response may be irrational rage. At other times, it may be calculated repression. The attackers must be expected to use whatever means they believe will be effective to halt, neutralize, or crush the resistance, as well as to inflict irrationally motivated brutalities. The civilian defenders must be prepared to withstand all such repression and to persist in their defense struggle.

Repression may be harsh. Resisters, their families, and their friends may be arrested, tortured, and killed. Whole population groups may be denied food, water, or fuel. Demonstrators, strikers, and obstructive civil servants may be shot. Mayors, city councillors, teachers, and clergy may be sent to concentration camps. Hostages taken to halt resistance may be executed.

The human costs of defense must not be underestimated. The casualties and other sacrifices in civilian-based defense need to be placed, however, in the context of the vastly higher costs of major conventional wars (the many millions in the First and Second World Wars, for example) and also the massive casualties which must be expected in any nuclear war. The costs of waging defense by civil resistance are in comparison very small indeed.

The defenders must not be surprised by severe repression and brutalities, and in response they must not halt their resistance. Flight or capitulation in face of the attackers' violence leads to defeat, not successful defense. Repression often follows recognition that the resisters' actions are indeed imperilling the success of the attack. Submission to repression will teach the attackers to repeat their violence in the future, for it will have proved to be effective in halting resistance.

The defenders must not capitulate to violence. They may, however, shift their particular strategy, tactics, and methods to others which continue to challenge the attackers equally strongly but do so in ways which reduce casualties. Suffering and deaths are virtually inevitable in acute struggles, including those waged by nonviolent means against violence. Nonviolent means do, however, tend to minimize casualties and destruction. Contrary to widespread impressions, the casualty rates for dead and wounded appear from the limited available evidence to be but a small fraction of those in roughly comparable conventional wars and especially of those in guerrilla wars.[12] When casualties occur in nonviolent struggle, they can bring the process of political 'jiu-jitsu' into operation, which in many cases can be crucial to producing success. In that process the opponents' violent repression actually works to undermine their power position by such means as provoking increased resistance, alienating third parties, and undermining support and arousing dissension among their own personnel and population.[13]

The weapons of civilian-based defense are nonviolent ones—political, social, economic, and psychological. Their success hinges in large part on persistence in applying them despite repression, while maintaining nonviolent discipline despite provocations. A shift to violence would alter the conflict from an asymmetrical one of nonviolent versus violent weapons—which has great advantages for the nonviolent civilian defenders—to a symmetrical one, in which both sides use violent weapons. That situation has great advantages for the attackers, who are normally well equipped to use violence. Violence from the side of civilian defenders disrupts the dynamics of nonviolent struggle, and weakens or even reverses the operation of mechanisms of change, especially the process of political 'jiu-jitsu'. Maintenance of nonviolent discipline is therefore a high priority.[14] In their past struggles against oppression and aggression, virtually all European peoples have experienced at certain points the need for maintaining nonviolent discipline in conflicts, as the Poles demonstrated during the struggles of the early 1980s. Advance preparations and training for civilian-based defense can increase the capacity of people to fulfil this and other requirements for maximizing its effectiveness.

INTERNATIONAL SUPPORT

Countries with civilian-based defense policies can in peacetime participate in a wide variety of international activities. They would not be isolationist simply because they lacked military alliances or military attack capacities, although they could make that choice. Many of the international activities of such countries would have little directly to do with deterrence and defense needs. For example, these countries might participate in United Nations and other multilateral efforts to alleviate pressing human needs, to improve nutrition and eradicate diseases, to protect nonliterate societies, to correct unfounded suspicions and misunderstandings, and to improve mutual understanding and friendship. These activities could reduce the number and intensity of future international conflicts. Those activities should be undertaken for their own sake, but they would increase the likelihood of major international support for a civilian-based defense country under attack.

International support could also be forthcoming on the basis of earlier arrangements and formal alliances, as discussed in Chapter 3. These could be bilateral or multilateral arrangements, a European Treaty Organization, a transformed North Atlantic Treaty Organization, regional organizations (such as the Nordic Council), or the United Nations and its various agencies.

Appropriate and potentially beneficial assistance to be arranged includes: printing and broadcasting facilities for the defending country; food and medical supplies; communication to the outside world of news about the defense struggle and the attackers' actions; mobilization of international economic and diplomatic sanctions against the aggression; communication with the attackers' troops and functionaries to provide them with news about the attack, the issues, repression, and resistance, and about dissent from the attackers' usual supporters; and, finally, pleas for assistance in ending the attack and in restoring international cooperation.

Such international aid is extremely important, but the main burden of the defense must be borne by the population of the attacked society itself. In civilian-based defense, no substitute exists for self-reliance, sound preparations, and genuine strength. European countries have demonstrated their capacities for both international assistance and self-reliance in peacetime and in wartime, including their often lonely resistance during Nazi, Russian, and other occupations. These societies are capable of waging this type of defense.

It must of course be recognized that some factors will enter into the struggle which are not under the control of either of the contesting groups. For example, unrelated international developments—such as a world economic downturn, an energy crisis, or the outbreak of conflict elsewhere—may influence the course of this struggle, sometimes to the detriment of the defenders and at other times to that of the aggressors. In cases in which the international dependency of either group is strong, that group's fortunes are likely to be seriously affected by the new developments, and a reassessment of its position will be required.

FAILURE AND SUCCESS

A civilian-based defense struggle may result in failure, success, or a mixture of the two. It is necessary to take a hard look at all of these, including the possibility of failure—just as the possibility of nuclear war has to be faced as a result of failure of nuclear deterrence.

The terms "success" and "failure" need to be used with clear meanings in discussing this policy.[15] This is necessary both to evaluate the effectivensss of any particular case of civilian-based defense and also to compare this policy with military policies generally.[16] "Success" in civilian-based defense is measured by the defenders' actually achieving their goals—that is, dissolving the attack and restoring their independent capacity to live by their own principles and institutions, with the ability to develop and change them as they may wish and to prevent future attacks. "Failure" therefore means that the defenders have not achieved their goals. In the case of a coup d'état, the attackers would have established and consolidated a new government. In the case of an invasion, the aggressors would have gained their objectives, probably including establishing political control.

The criteria for evaluating success and failure are therefore more complex than whether the enemy has been physically destroyed or has capitulated to superior military forces. The terms "success" and "failure" and "victory" and "defeat" are thus used to convey meanings of political substance in relation to this policy.

This ought also to be the practice in relation to military conflicts, but it is generally not so. Instead, in those cases the terms are used to convey simply military ascendancy and submission related to the relative distribution of the physical destruction and death inflicted by each side on the other. Military victory or defeat may or may not result in achieving or losing the original objectives of the conflict. Those objectives tend to be neglected in favor of the military outcome.

Not every attempt to apply civilian-based defense will succeed. Its requirements for effectiveness must be fulfilled if success is to follow. In wars, military defeat is likely to have been caused by vast physical destruction, loss of life, and demoralization (with a perceived inability to continue the struggle to a successful conclusion). These conditions can also accompany failure in civilian-based defense, but this is less likely.

To the degree that the resistance spirit and the resilience of the society's independent institutions are maintained, the population can renew the defense struggle at a later time. In the interim, rest may-be required. This can be a period for renewing the society's strength and capacity to rebound, developing new strategies, and choosing new achievable, specific goals for selective resistance.

In other words, definitive defeat in civilian-based defense need never exist as long as the society survives.

In addition to such periods of rest, there will be times to regroup defense capacities. Stages will occur in which one side or the other gains or loses strength and achieves more or less of its immediate objectives. During stages when the attackers are in the ascendancy the civilian defenders may be required to endure great suffering and casualties. As long as they maintain their will, however, they can strengthen themselves and their institutions and refine their skills in applying nonviolent struggle. The defenders can increase their courage and persistence in the face of struggle to create new defense situations more favorable to their cause. These changes will progressively strengthen the defenders, weaken the attackers, and achieve the goals for which the struggle is waged: defeating the attackers' venture and aims.

Measuring success and failure by the achievement or nonachievement of the attackers' and defenders' respective goals soon reveals that the outcomes of many struggles are mixtures of success and failure. When this is the case, it is important that the civilian defenders realize their achievements and strengths. Sometimes people have fought well by nonviolent struggle and have gained significant objectives. However, because they had not yet achieved full success, they thought themselves defeated. They therefore sometimes capitulated, defeating themselves. That can be avoided. The defenders can learn to recognize their accomplishments and evaluate more objectively the degree of success and failure achieved at any point.

When degrees of success and failure exist, the civilian defenders' responsibility is to increase the internal strength of their own society. They need to identify and apply their relevant power leverages on the attackers, improve their skill and strategic judgment, and focus resistance on the attackers' weak points. They then need to act with deliberation, courage, and steadfastness in order to achieve complete success.

Civilian-based defense can also produce full success for the defenders. A sequence of selective resistance campaigns can result in a series of losses for the attackers and gains for the defenders. These may cause the aggressors to become weaker, while the defenders grow in strength and move progressively closer to success.

Some defense struggles will bring victory in undramatic ways and perhaps even involve negotiations and some face-saving formula to enable the invaders to withdraw with reduced humiliation, as mentioned earlier. Other struggles, however, will be fought out to an unmistakable conclusion.

The difficulties encountered by the attackers—when they are confronted by well-prepared, sophisticated civilian defenders—must not be underestimated. Civilian defenders should be able to frustrate and finally defeat their adversaries, given real internal strength in their society, strategic and tactical wisdom, discipline and persistence in the face of provocation and repression, and ability to capitalize on their own strengths while striking at the attackers' weaknesses.

The attackers may find their goals denied, their orders and policies unimplemented, and their attempts to crush resistance to have not only failed but backfired. The results are less—rather than more—control and increased resistance. The attackers' attempts to centralize command in their own hands are blocked by the persistent and increasing autonomy of the society. The reliability of their own troops and functionaries becomes more and more threatened, as they become confused, disillusioned, resentful, and finally unreliable and mutinous. Even the attackers' home population gradually begins to dissent and to oppose the aggression. Members of the international community increasingly shift from vocal condemnation to economic, political, and diplomatic sanctions.

The attackers, long confident that sufficient violence will achieve their goals, may become bewildered and angry when their policies and repression fail. When more severe repression also fails, brutalities may be inflicted on the resisting population, only to accelerate the process of political 'jiu-jitsu'. Rational and flexible attackers may then seek to extricate themselves from the situation, with minimal damage and perhaps some gains. However, more determined and rigid opponents may persist in their ever more unsuccessful and counter-productive efforts, until the whole venture unravels.

On occasion, the defenders may then adjust their strategy towards increasingly general resistance and total noncooperation to provide a knockout blow to the aggression: a full economic shut-down, intensive subversion of the attackers' troops, major international sanctions (as an oil embargo or undermining of the attackers' currency), or establishment or major expansion of a full parallel government. On other occasions, different concluding strategies may be needed.

In the last stages of struggle, the defenders tend to become increasingly autonomous and strong, while the attackers' camp may become filled with growing dissension and weakness.[17] The attackers will be forced to withdraw. The attack will have been dissolved, leaving the people of the defending society with their independence and chosen way of life and institutions restored, and their future in their own hands.

7 ASSESSING THE POTENTIAL

STEPS IN CONSIDERATION AND ADOPTION

Civilian-based defense requires time for its investigation, development, and consideration. It is in most countries unlikely to be adopted quickly, although the steps in that direction could proceed far more rapidly than most people imagine.

Several scenarios have been suggested, in broad terms, to project the process by which a change-over to the policy might occur. None of these has been worked out or critically examined as fully as is desirable. The process of change-over accepted in this book as most likely to be successful is the incremental approach. That means that, instead of a dramatically quick acceptance of the new policy, its development, evaluation, and acceptance will be achieved as the result of a series of steps, some small and others larger.[1]

At times these will be very small ones, simply involving recognition that nonviolent forms of struggle can, at least sometimes, cause difficulties for aggressors and oppressors. Since that recognition will not come simultaneously or equally to all persons and groups in the society, many small steps may reflect and contribute to that new perception.

At a more advanced stage it may be accepted that the possibility of such a defense merits research, further development, or a feasibility study for a very limited situation—as when military means have already been used and been crushed. Even if research is proposed by skeptics as a delaying tactic to block actual consideration of the policy, that research is an advance for it involves the political system in the investigation of civilian-based defense and enlarges knowledge and understanding about it.

Another limited, but more advanced, step is to add a very small nonviolent resistance component to an overwhelmingly military security policy. Then, in another significant incremental step, that established small component could be refined and enlarged by introducing serious preparations and training of the population, and by establishing guidelines for resistance by the society's institutions. Many other smaller steps could precede or occur alongside these, such as study and evaluation of the policy by the society's social, military, trade union, business, political, and religious organizations.

Once a serious, well-founded civilian-based defense component is a viable part of the over-all security policy of the society, it might remain only that. However, if despite earlier doubts and reservations the new component comes to be seen by much of the society to be powerful and to possess significant advantages over military means, it could be expanded. Civilian-based defense could then become a proportionately larger slice of the whole defense "pie." In time, the society could potentially scale down, and perhaps eventually phase out, reliance on military means. In comparison to the new policy they might be seen to be excessively dangerous, ineffective for real defense, or even counterproductive.[2]

There are other views of how a shift to nonviolent means of national defense might occur. Some people see such a change as necessarily following some type of conversion to a moral rejection of violence. Others see a change in defense as necessarily following successful fundamental social, economic, and political change to a more equalitarian and participatory system. Some people doubt that a shift to nonviolent means of defense will come unless in response to some horrendous, perhaps nuclear, military disaster. This is not the place for a fuller presentation of those views or for the substantive criticism which can lead to their rejection.[3]

With the incrementalist conception of change-over, a large series of achievable small steps toward adoption of civilian-based defense not only become possible. They also may become stages in the progressive recognition and acceptance of civilian-based defense as a preferred and viable policy to prevent and defend against attack.

In various European countries some of the limited steps mentioned above have already taken place. In the incrementalist view of change to the new policy, the significance of those developments may be much greater than would otherwise be understood.

Even if an official government committee rejects the civilian-based defense policy completely, that rejection is an advance because the policy had never been previously officially considered, and a second and third official examination of it would from that point on become quite possible. If a government policy document on defense rejects the nonviolent policy as incapable of deterring aggression, but reluctantly accepts that civilian-based defense merits further attention for possible last-ditch resistance against an overwhelming superior military power, that is an advance. It is a recognition that nonviolent forms of struggle may be able to persist where military means have been crushed. Similar situations may exist for other apparently negative judgments. All such steps may lead to further development and consideration of the policy, which may help to make it more effective and to be recognized as such.

A word of caution is merited here, however. Adoption of an incrementalist approach is not a guarantee of quick, easy, or continuous progress toward adoption of the policy. A process of consideration may move forward, even rapidly, for a while, only to come to a halt for a significant period of time (as happened, for example, in Finland). In another case, after a period of growing consideration of the policy, the continuing investigation may level off at a very low point for some time. This has been illustrated by the consideration of the policy in the Netherlands. Such a halt, or slowing, of consideration could arise from various causes. It may, however, be especially likely when the exploration has not grown from a nonpartisan search for alternatives but instead has been pressed by certain movements or political groups regarded by major sections of the society as too extreme, anti-military, or ideological. As a consequence, the opponents of those groups may without serious examination reject the civilian-based defense policy simply because they reject its proponents. Then, when political fortunes shift, the policy is then set aside along with the rejected groups and defeated parties which had espoused it.

In short, it may be extremely important to involve conservatives, pro-military groups, military officers, and other sections of the society which might be thought to be unsympathetic to the concept of civilian-based defense in the actual consideration and investigation of the policy. This is for a variety of reasons. If influential persons and groups among them conclude that the policy should be explored and may have some merit, the favorable impact of this on opinions of others in the society may be significant. Another reason for this approach is to facilitate a more even advance in the development, investigation and consideration of the policy by the society as a whole, avoiding halts and slowing of the process. In addition, this strategy will help to ensure that if and when the time comes for actual adoption of the policy, it will not be in a polarized society, with major groups determined to reject it or even support a coup d'état to prevent its adoption. Instead, the new policy will have the backing and participation of the society as a whole which is necessary for its effectiveness and credibility.

Where a halt or slowing in consideration of the policy has occurred this need not necessarily end the process of exploration. The steps already taken may remain significant and, given new stimuli and conditions, a fresh exploration may start the process again, perhaps on more of a nonpartisan basis.

Let us now survey very briefly the possible relevance of civilian-based defense for the countries of Western Europe and the status of elements of the policy in some of them. We will first focus on the nonaligned or permanently neutral countries, and then on the countries which are members of NATO.

CIVILIAN-BASED DEFENSE FOR NONALIGNED COUNTRIES?

Well-prepared nonaligned and permanently neutral countries could in at least some cases wage a serious fight by conventional military means against a Soviet attack. Recall Finland's defensive Winter War of 1939–1940 against the USSR, or consider Sweden's present impressive conventional military forces. It is a virtual certainty, however, that a determined Soviet attack would defeat the military defenders.

This raises two serious questions for defense planners in such countries: "What then, after heroic but defeated military resistance?" and "Could defenders of nonaligned countries increase their chances of deterring a Soviet attack and, if attacked, of successfully defending their country, by fighting instead with nonconventional means?"

Several European countries which are independent of the North Atlantic and the Warsaw Pact alliances have sought answers to such questions. These include Switzerland, Austria, Finland, Yugoslavia, and Sweden. Except, perhaps, for Yugoslavia, all of these continue to place strongest confidence in conventional military forces and weaponry. The limitations of that capacity against far more powerful military enemies is in each case implicitly and even explicitly recognized, however. All these countries envisage the time when further conventional frontal military action against an invader might be impossible, and nonconventional means of struggle would be the only way to avoid capitulation. That may not be a pleasant prospect, but it has more chance of avoiding nuclear annihilation than does NATO's strategy, and it does represent the honesty of seeking ways to deal with situations one would prefer to avoid.

These nonaligned countries have faced the possibility that they may be unable to keep the attackers' forces out of their own territory—a sobering but salutary recognition of reality. They have all, therefore, deliberately planned ways to continue the struggle in face of hostile military forces inside their country—a wiser choice than resorting to nuclear weapons in that contingency. The capacity to wage effective struggle against the attackers in one's own country is seen as also serving as a deterrent to attack. These policies thus share significant characteristics with civilian-based defense. Each of these nonaligned countries has adopted defense policies which include in addition to conventional military means both paramilitary and nonmilitary means of struggle. The complete policy in these cases is then variously labeled as "total defense" or "general defense," to indicate that it is something much more than conventional military weaponry and forces.

Switzerland's "general defense" policy includes military means, civil defense, guerrilla struggle, nonviolent resistance, political means, diplomatic measures, and ideological countermeasures. Austria's "general national defense" policy includes psychological, civil, and economic defense, as well as military means, with both conventional and guerrilla strategies to operate within Austrian territory. Finland's security policy places major emphasis on its foreign policy as well as defense policy, with the latter including conventional military forces, within the framework of a territorial system of defense, guerrilla struggle in occupied areas, along with economic defense, civil defense, defense information for the home population, and maintenance of public order, communications, and medical services. Yugoslavia's "total national defense" policy includes conventional military capacity, territorial defense, "unarmed forms of struggle and resistance" (which include both violent and nonviolent means, among the latter boycotts and noncollaboration), and civil defense. Sweden's "total defense" policy includes in addition to conventional military components psychological defense, economic defense, civil defense, medical services, communications, and emergency administration.

These countries have thus broken both from the pretense that it is possible to keep the attackers' forces and weapons out of one's country and from the presumption that (among nonnuclear options) only conventional military weaponry, forces, and strategies can provide serious defense capacities. These insights make their policies far more sophisticated than those of most countries. Their policies are also predominantly defensive, without a significant capacity to attack or counterattack other countries.

These three elements—acceptance of nonconventional means of struggle, recognition that the weapons and forces of attackers are likely to enter the country, and choice of predominantly defensive policies—open the way for the recognition by these countries of the importance of civilian-based defense and of the need to develop and evaluate its potential for meeting their defense needs. All these countries either now have some type of nonviolent resistance component within their national defense policies or have initiated some type of consideration of that possibility. There have been compelling reasons for nonaligned and permanently neutral countries, dependent on their own resources, at least to add a minimal civil resistance component alongside their military capacities. The question becomes whether, to what degree, and in what ways that component will be made more explicit and expanded.[4]

CIVILIAN-BASED DEFENSE FOR NATO COUNTRIES?

A rapid shift from present NATO policies by the alliance as a whole or by individual members to full civilian-based defense is most unlikely. This is also true of all major military systems. However, significant beginnings can be taken without a decision to transarm completely. Those beginnings can contribute to enhanced security, and should receive the support of persons and groups which would oppose more dramatic shifts. Yet those limited steps may become moves toward full transarmament. As has been suggested, the beginnings are likely to be in research, policy and feasibility studies, and education. From them it would be relatively simple to move to public evaluation, consideration by the non-governmental institutions in the societies, and policy examination of the potential by individual governments and perhaps even the alliance. Following such groundwork, decisions could be made to initiate and then expand preparations and training to build up the deterrence and defense capacity.

Far short of full transarmament, civilian-based defense could be adopted initially by the whole alliance or by individual member countries to meet specific limited needs. For example, civilian-based defense measures could be reserved for deterring and defeating coups d'état, or for continuing resistance in case of military occupation following retreat or defeat in military warfare. Such a limited step does not lead inevitably to full adoption of the policy: selective adoption might be halted at a certain point (or even reversed).

However, given a judgment of effectiveness, the role of the new policy might be gradually expanded by several incremental steps. At a later time, the policy might be deemed adequate to replace military means completely, and a phased process of full transarmament could be implemented. That would mean that the European countries would no longer "require" American or European nuclear weapons for deterrence or combat use. While political ties with the United States could continue, the European countries would be self-reliant in their security policies.

That would largely lift the dangers of nuclear destruction of Europe and make Western European countries unlikely to become victims of internal or foreign aggression.

There are factors now operating in European countries that may accelerate consideration of civilian-based defense. They include: the growth of popular interest in the policy; the expanding recognition of the extreme dangers of present nuclear weapons policies; the continuing resistance in Poland; the appearance of sophisticated country-specific discussions of the policy along with strictly defensive military options (such as the British Alternative Defence Commission's 'Defence Without the Bomb';[5] the beginnings of inclusion of the policy in the official positions of political parties;[6] and early cases of small-scale governmental examination, which began in 1967 and have occurred in one way or another in Denmark, Norway, Sweden, Finland, and the Netherlands.

One major focal point for investigation by both non-aligned and NATO countries is the likely effectiveness, or lack of it, of civilian-based defense against possible attack by the Soviet Union. The following discussion is offered as a contribution to those more detailed analyses which must be made for each individual country.

DANGERS FOR THE SOVIET UNION

Significant grounds exist for believing that the Soviet Union could be deterred by prepared civilian-based defense policies in Western European countries, and further that this policy could defeat the Soviet Union if it did invade, preventing it from securing its objectives and from consolidating control.

Since 1953 the Soviet Union has repeatedly been confronted by spontaneous and improvised nonviolent struggle in various Eastern European countries. Although it has been able by military means to put down such movements and revolutions, it has been unable to halt their continuing development. The first prominent case—the June 1953 East German Rising—was subdued after two days. The Hungarian Revolution of 1956–1957—with two nonviolent phases and one military—lasted four months. Czechoslovak improvised nonviolent resistance to the Soviet and Warsaw Pact invasion and occupation held off achievement of the Soviet objective of a compliant, hard-line regime for eight months. The democratization movement in Poland, from the organization of Solidarity through the resistance to martial law and later controls of the military regime has now continued as a powerful force for more than four years (at this writing). The nonviolent challenges are becoming more serious and it is taking the Soviet Union significantly longer to overcome each one.

Thus Soviet difficulties in controlling past and present improvised nonviolent struggle have been very considerable. But preparations and training for civilian-based defense would increase the potential power of such resistance well beyond that in those improvised cases. As experienced practitioners and analysts of power politics, the Soviet leadership could be expected to respond with appropriate caution.

The impact on the morale of Soviet troops carrying out repression on nonviolent resisters in East Germany, Hungary, and Czechoslovakia was also considerable, leading at times to large-scale unreliability and troop replacement, and at other times to limited mutinies. In the case of Poland, the Soviet Union wisely kept Soviet troops out and relied on Polish troops, perhaps having learned from the Czechoslovak experience, and perhaps because of morale, discipline, and desertion problems among prospective invasion troops. (The general reliability of Polish troops during martial law requires study.) The Soviet morale and discipline problems in these several cases would be vastly aggravated by civilian-based defense, in which major preparations would have been made for deliberate subversion of occupation troops.

The Russian Empire and the Soviet Union have long been xenophobic. Major efforts have been made to keep all foreign influences out completely, or strictly control them. A large-scale Soviet invasion of Western Europe would bring hundreds of thousands of ordinary soldiers, officers, and functionaries into direct contact with Western European ways of life and with especially "dangerous" populations. That would be particularly true following transarmament to civilian-based defense. While not threatening the troops physically, the Western European populations would be firmly opposed to the Soviet system and its domination. They not only would believe strongly in their own society and their right to improve it themselves, but would be trained in how to subvert the loyalties of the invading personnel while resisting the occupation itself. This prospect would be likely to evoke great caution, if not terror, in the Soviet policy makers.

The difficulties and dilemmas of repressing nonviolent struggle are daunting. These would very likely create grave problems in making decisions on policies and stimulate conflicts among the Soviet leadership, as reportedly occurred in the cases of Hungary and Poland, as well as aggravating any existing problems.

Even within a military contest, there is strong evidence that the Soviet military forces suffer from inflexibility as their most serious military shortcoming: inability to make adjustments (even under orders) in the original plans; inability of lower-level units to exercise creativity and initiative when cut off from their commands; and inability to adjust action to meet unanticipated conditions and actions.[7] Since civilian-based defense would bring invading Soviet

troops into intimate and continuing contact with defending populations waging a defense which produces constant changes in the situation and takes forms for which advance orders to troops could never
be fully adequate, the Soviet military forces may be especially vulnerable to civilian-based defense.

Invasion and occupation of countries which posed no military
threat to the Soviet Union, as a result of their transarmament to civilian-based defense, could produce major international political costs
for the Soviet leaders. (The impact of these costs should not be exaggerated since the Soviet Union has been willing to pay them in the
past in various cases of aggression. The point is simply that the costs
exist and would have to be carefully evaluated, along with other factors discussed here which are likely to be more decisive.)

These political costs could be expected to be imposed not only by
clearly anti-Communist governments, but also by Third World countries and at the United Nations. This could imperil established trade
relations and economic or military cooperation. Judging from experience in the cases of Hungary, Czechoslovakia, Poland, and Afghanistan, various Communist parties could also be expected to denounce
any such invasion and occupation. The costs might also include dete-
rioration of relations with China and other Communist states. The
Soviet Union has been willing to suffer such losses previously but,
added to other serious costs and defeats, such a decline in influence
and goodwill would be significant.

In Czechoslovakia the Communist Party itself became for some
time a resistance organization against the Soviet invasion and occupation. Communists in Hungary and Poland have joined the movements
for change and opposition to submission to the Soviet Union. Considering the emergence of Eurocommunism and the greater independence of several Communist parties (in Italy, for example) from
Soviet influence, a Soviet invasion of Western European countries
with civilian-based defense policies would probably be opposed by
most Communists in those countries, as well as by the rest of the
population. Powerful resistance by civilian-based defense against such
an invasion of Western Europe might also trigger nonviolent uprisings
for liberation in Eastern Europe, which the USSR considers vital to
its security.

Massive invasions of Western European countries by the Soviet
Union would be very costly economically and potentially disruptive
to Soviet domestic and international economic arrangements. That

could be extremely damaging in light of the existing weaknesses of the Soviet economy and its dependence on the West for grain.

Potentially most serious of all is the contagion effect of non-violent struggle on the Soviet Union itself and on other countries under its influence and control. In the past nonviolent struggle has often spread by imitation. In the future, not only news reports from other countries and hearsay, but also such deliberate means as foreign radio broadcasts, leaflets, books, newspapers, and tape recordings, can teach new populations about this type of action and specific methods. Strikes, fasts, sitdowns, and economic boycotts have all spread by imitation in earlier decades. Soviet censorship could work only for a time.

The hundreds of thousands of Soviet personnel required to invade and occupy Western European countries with civilian-based defense policies would eventually return home. Despite controls and delaying tactics, these people would eventually come into contact with friends, relatives, and the general populace. Stories of what had occurred in Western Europe would be told, including how the resistance had been waged and the difficulties it posed to the occupation officials.

In time, that new knowledge of how to struggle, perhaps combined with other information and creative innovation, could spread. The results would be adverse for the Soviet leadership. The history of the Russian Empire and the Soviet Union includes not only autocracy and Communist dictatorship but also struggles for freedom. These include the great 1905 predominantly nonviolent revolution and the February 1917 revolution, also largely nonviolent.

The spread of knowledge of how to wage nonviolent struggle might affect significantly the many potentially dissident nationalities now ruled by the Great Russians, themselves only a slight majority of the total USSR population. There is historical precedent for such a development. During the 1905 Revolution against the tsarist system, various nationalities broke completely from the Empire's control, and established independent governments which in some cases were not reconquered for many months. In the future the grasping of a more sophisticated understanding of nonviolent struggle could lead to the disintegration of the Soviet Union into its constituent nationalities.

Spread of knowledge of nonviolent struggle could also aid struggles for greater freedom by Great Russians themselves. Students, the intelligentsia, workers, peasants, and religious groups are likely to be particularly interested. The new knowledge might help to transform dissatisfaction without hope of change into determination to struggle with confidence based on knowledge of how to do so. The Soviet Union's general population may be quite open to using nonviolent struggle, as the Eastern Europeans have been. This would be an unwanted consequence of a Soviet invasion of Western European countries prepared to wage civilian-based defense.

Wise Soviet leadership should, for such reasons as these, forget the idea of invading countries with civilian-based defense policies. If such invasions were nevertheless launched, because of overconfidence in the capacity of military action, for example, the Soviet leaders ought, in their own interests, to expedite a withdrawal. The power realities of this policy sooner or later force their own recognition, even from reluctant rulers.

COSTS OF CIVILIAN-BASED DEFENSE

Every possible policy to increase Western European security has costs. Some of these already exist and can therefore be calculated and examined with a reasonable degree of certainty. Some are potential costs, which may or may not be incurred, but must be considered. No careful cost analyses have yet been made for civilian-based defense for particular countries. It is clear, however, that both the type and level of costs would vary with the particular country, the stage of transarmament, whether the new policy was added alongside the military capacity or had become a full substitute, and whether the country was self-reliant or a member of an alliance.

A serious cost of any deterrence and defense policy is the price in disruption, destruction, injury, and death which may be required in open conflict, when deterrence has failed (as already discussed). It is important to remember that this type of cost for civilian-based defense, while appreciable, is relatively modest, compared to that which would be incurred as a result of the failure of deterrence by either conventional military or nuclear options. With this policy the cost is one of a continuing defense struggle, with relatively limited casualties. This allows life to continue and offers the serious prospect of liberation by defeat of the aggressors.

The most serious cost of the civilian-based defense policy would be incurred if it failed both as deterrent and as defense. The possibility of its failure has been discussed in the previous chapter. Those costs should, of course, be compared to the costs of surrender and of failure of conventional and nuclear weapons both to deter and to defend.

The economic costs of the preparations for civilian-based defense and of its practice would be far less than those of military policies. The trend is clearly for the cost of military hardware to increase very substantially. Even the largest states are already affected by the economic impact of this. During the initial transition period of transarmament, however, the costs of preparations for the new policy would be added to those of the continuing military policy: money, resources, and personnel would be required for both. Total defense expenditures could increase temporarily, or they might decrease in cases where new expensive military weapons systems were not procured or where other major military budget cuts were possible. After the transition period, the costs of civilian-based defense would depend on the extent to which the society shifted to this policy.

If the society chose to maintain both policies side by side for an indefinite period, then obviously costs would be incurred for both, although the levels of each could vary widely. If the society chose to transarm fully, the regular costs for civilian-based defense preparations alone would eventually be very low, as compared to previous military costs. While there have been no estimates of such costs, a very rough estimate is that they would be no more than 10 percent of the previous military costs and possibly significantly lower.

Among the factors incurring costs for civilian-based defense in money, resources, productive capacity, and human assistance are research, policy studies, preparations, training, and maneuvers. These costs would include full-time and part-time staff, possible release time from work for job-related defense training, equipment (printing, broadcasting, etc.), training books and films, food storage, and other physical requirements. Maneuvers—exercises to act out resistance plans—conducted for massive training would periodically involve the loss of economic production for a day or two. If economic, population, energy, or institutional decentralization were deemed necessary to increase defense effectiveness, those costs might be high in the short run, though possibly cheaper in the long run.

In societies with serious internal problems—such as poverty, alienation, and perceived oppression—the chances of collaboration with the attackers would be increased. This would heighten the likelihood of defeat. The population's will to defend and its solidarity in a crisis would in such cases be strengthened by programs to remove those grievances. Their removal would enlarge the degree of democracy and the defense potential. Such programs would, of course, have initial economic costs, but these could be met from the savings in military expenditures.

Where special arrangements or alliances do not provide (or no longer provide) intelligence about the troop movements of potential attackers, or similar data, the provision of substitute personnel and equipment (as spy satellites) to gather such information would incur additional costs.

When this policy is successfully applied for defense against invasion and occupation and restores independence and secures withdrawal of the invaders, additional costs might still be incurred. Resources might be required to assist the resettlement of the attackers' troops and other personnel who had mutinied during the conflict and feared punishment if they returned home prior to a change of government. A little imagination will suggest other costs.

If a world military power were to transarm fully, it would no longer be able to intervene militarily in other parts of the world. This change would be evaluated differently by various elements of the society. Some would count it as a benefit, by reducing chances of involvement in world-wide wars. Others might see the loss of military intervention capacity as a loss of influence and prestige. However, transarmament may in the initial cases create new sources of influence and prestige based on the pioneering role of the civilian-based defense country in developing the new policy. Loss of the ability to intervene militarily in other parts of the world is not a relevant factor for most countries of Western Europe, but it would be for Britain and France.

The economic and technological implications of the long-term dismantling of military-based industries of some sections of the Western European economy could be highly positive. It could free resources, industrial capacity, research facilities and funds, and personnel for technological innovation and production of civilian goods.

Other costs might accrue to NATO members which transarmed. These could include loss of goodwill with the United States, political and economic costs, and a sense of separation. Whether these actually occur, or are serious, will depend heavily on how the transition is handled by both the individual country and the United States. Therefore, it is important that the American public and policy makers understand in advance the nature and capacities of this defense policy and its advantages for providing Western European security while reducing the costs and dangers for the United States.

If the United States government had no confidence in the new policy for its European allies, and during the years of transarmament consistently opposed the preparations and change, those costs might be high. If the diplomatic and strategic discussions between the European countries and the United States about the new policy were not handled well, the result could be a long-term loss of goodwill between them. Conversely, educational work in the United States and efforts by the transarming European countries could lead to positive understanding and recognition of the mutual advantages of the new policy, along with continued goodwill, enhanced by the ending of the dependency relationship.

Another cost to transarmed European countries would be that of bearing full responsibility for their own defense. No longer could a major part of that burden be shifted to the United States. Some NATO members might find difficulties in accepting that responsibility. However, the overall burden would quite likely become lighter, with recognition of the drastic reduction of the dangers of conventional and nuclear war in Europe.

The increased responsibility of each country for its own defense could be accompanied by growing self-determination and pride. The possible sense of separation from former supporters and allies could be minimized or eliminated by special mutual aid treaty arrangements or transarmament of NATO itself, in part or in full, as discussed in Chapter 3. Economic costs of the new policy could also be shared in these ways, although except in the transition period that should be unnecessary since civilian-based defense is much less costly than military forces and weapons.

Some costs of the new policy might be internal ones. Spreading knowledge of how to apply nonviolent struggle for defense would make that information available to groups within the country with grievances against the government, the society, or a section of the society. Such groups would therefore be more likely to use these methods than they would have previously. Some people would regard that use as an additional cost. In Europe this could include increased nonviolent struggle by economically marginal groups, racial and language minorities, and nationalities seeking greater autonomy or outright secession.

Two factors need to be considered here in evaluating the seriousness of that cost, or whether it is a cost. First, a society claiming adherence to the principles of freedom and democracy widely espoused in Europe ought to be grateful for such stimuli, especially when they can preclude the rise of terrorist movements. These nonviolent stimuli could help the society remove legitimate grievances of parts of its population. Their removal would not only improve the society and bring it closer to the espoused principles. It would also increase the future solidarity of the country against attacks, by removing grounds for indifference to them or even for collaboration with an enemy who promises enticing changes.

In addition to potential costs of transarmament to civilian-based defense, there are also a series of possible benefits and also other significant domestic and international consequences, many of them positive.

POTENTIAL BENEFITS AND CONSEQUENCES

The process of transarmament would be likely to produce various benefits for the society, as well as wider changes in the international system. The extent of these benefits and changes would be influenced by the characteristics of the particular case of transarmament. Partial transarmament, for example, would have fewer fundamental consequences for improving international security or for fostering domestic social change than would full transarmament. Full transarmament by a single small country which had stayed out of Europe's wider problems—as has Switzerland—would have much less initial impact on European security than would transarmament by West Germany or France. Transarmament by several countries, acting independently or by agreement, would probably have significantly more impact than transarmament by a single country.

The quality and extent of civilian-based defense preparations are also important. If they are weak and inadequate, they might discredit the policy. This is especially the case if this happens in the first countries to transarm and they are then invaded and defeated. On the other hand, if the first countries prepare well and develop strong capacities, they are likely to deter possible attacks and in crises to defeat them more quickly than observers might expect. That could encourage wider adoption of civilian-based defense in Europe.

While the policy is designed to operate in the contemporary political world with all its dangers, it contributes to basic changes toward more desirable domestic and international systems. Some of these changes result from removing certain influences of military systems and war, while others are derivative of the nature of the alternative policy.

Military organizations, originally intended for national security, can be turned against the domestic political system and carry out a coup d'état. A civilian-based defense system cannot do this since it requires mass participation of the population and its institutions, not simply efficient action by military officers and their subordinates. Hence, the new policy is more compatible with parliamentary government than are military systems. In addition, civilian-based defense, as discussed in Chapters 4, 5, and 6 has a deterrence and defense capability against coups d'état, and other internal usurpations.

Civilian-based defense is also likely to reduce internal violence and terrorism by dissenting groups. The shift from military to nonviolent sanctions for defense will contribute to the delegitimizing of violence as the ultimate sanction of the society.[8] In its place, nonviolent forms of struggle will be increasingly seen as the legitimate and appropriate technique for waging extreme conflicts. Those are ones in which compromise is believed to be impossible, or the milder procedural means of conflict resolution (as negotiations, arbitration, seeking legislation, or court decisions) are not seen to be appropriate or adequate.

In other words, there is likely to be less terrorism and more civil disobedience and hunger strikes as means of expressing dissent and struggling for causes. Western European societies have had sufficient experience with terrorism and other types of political violence by groups claiming legitimate grievances or noble causes that these societies may, despite irritations and minor disruptions, be grateful and responsive when such groups apply nonviolent action. From the dissenters' view, a shift from terrorism to nonviolent action may prove to be the most effective way to bring sympathetic attention to the grievance, while minimizing repression. From the society's view, the shift may prove the most effective way to remove the problem of terrorism.

Civilian-based defense would not involve the huge expenditures required by modern military hardware. This is because the defense responsibilities are primarily shifted from expensive technology to the general population and the society's independent institutions. This could have two significant effects, one economic and the other political.

Economically, the shift could open the way for conscious economic changes toward meeting human needs more adequately and considering environmental factors more fully. These moves would make more economic resources available for domestic civilian needs and for international assistance, where appropriate.

Politically, the drastic reduction of expenditures for deterrence and defense—achieved by the replacement of massive military systems and weapons technology with defense preparations by the general population and the society's civil institutions—would dramatically diminish the size of government. This is the key to reversing the immense growth of modern state power.

Civilian-based defense would also remove the centralizing influences endemic to military systems and introduce the decentralizing influences associated with nonviolent sanctions.[9] These would together contribute to the development of a less centralist and more pluralist social and political structure, with greater popular participation.

Major social change is not, however, required in any of the constitutional democracies of Europe before they can begin to transarm to civilian-based defense. However, calculations of the conditions which would likely increase the effectiveness of future defense struggles may suggest the need for certain changes as that process continues. These changes are likely deliberately to reverse present trends toward economic and political centralization, and to move toward diffusion and devolution of power, control, and production. These shifts will require technology appropriate to decentralization and to the reduction of the scale of institutions generally, specifically those of economic production and distribution and of politics.[10]

The process of considering civilian-based defense, preparing for it, and placing responsibility for defense on people themselves, would encourage citizens to think about certain important matters more than they do at present. People would be more likely to recognize and evaluate freshly the principles, institutions, and qualities of the society which are worthy of defense. This could lead to increased commitment to them, to applying those principles more fully to make the society more just and free, and to increasing popular participation in democratic life in peacetime. This would both enrich the society and increase the people's will and capacity to resist aggressors and usurpers.

Civilian-based defense is also likely to contribute to the development of a more "positive" foreign policy and interest in other parts of the world. On the one hand, the defense policy is freed from military requirements, allocation of resources for military purposes, and military alliances with dictatorships and other distasteful regimes. On the other, the new policy may be made more effective by measures which today are justified largely on grounds of altruism, and are either irrelevant to, or in competition with, present national security requirements.

With civilian-based defense, however, it will be advantageous to the defense and security interests of one's own society to help to meet human needs in other countries, resolve international problems short of open conflict, and win international goodwill by merit. That goodwill is needed because the support of other countries can be helpful in case the civilian-based defense country is attacked. The transarmed country, for its own interest as well as that of others, may also encourage other countries to consider civilian-based defense and assist them in exploring it. Should they choose to transarm in part or in full, the country already transarmed could assist them in planning their preparations and training.

The population of a transarmed country would also benefit from learning more about other societies, languages, cultures, and systems, and about the problems and aspirations of other peoples. In peacetime a civilian-based defense society with such knowledge and understanding will be more likely to work with people in other societies to remove problems and meet needs which, if neglected, might fuel future international crises. On the one hand, this may contribute to greater international understanding and goodwill. On the other, in case the civilian-based defense country is invaded, its people will be more able to communicate with and subvert the occupation troops and functionaries.

Transarmament in Western Europe would affect Eastern Europe, even without deliberate Western efforts to promote nonviolent struggle there. Political contagion tends to spread the use of nonviolent forms of struggle among populations that regard themselves as oppressed. An inter-stimulation process can occur between Western Europeans transarming to civilian-based defense and Eastern Europeans seeking liberation from Communist rule and general Soviet hegemony.

At present Western Europeans have more to learn from Eastern European experience with nonviolent struggle in their various movements since 1953 than Eastern Europeans have to learn from the peoples of Western Europe. However, with research, policy studies, preparations, training, and phased transarmament programs, the Swedes, Norwegians, Danes, Germans, Dutch, French, Belgians, and all the rest—by their individual and collective efforts—may soon have available much from which freedom-minded Eastern Europeans can learn. News of transarmament preparations, reports of training maneuvers, and copies of handbooks are likely to have a significant impact in increasing the Eastern Europeans' future skills in waging nonviolent struggle, even without deliberate Western efforts to inform those populations about the new policy.

The development of civilian-based defense in Western Europe will contribute to a broader process of growing capacities to prevent and remove dictatorships. In addition to the direct contributions of this policy discussed in previous chapters, civilian-based defense would enlarge our understanding of how to undermine an existing dictatorship and how to assist people of another country struggling against a dictatorial system or an attempt to impose one. Other aspects of dictatorship prevention would include increasing our knowledge of how to structure the society so as to facilitate free democratic political institutions, how to make it difficult or impossible to impose a dictatorship, and also how to achieve greater social justice without using dictatorial means.[11] Developing these capabilities is likely to have, in the long run, major international significance. This is important for Third World countries, where at present the societies are demonstrably highly vulnerable to coups d'état, dictatorial regimes, and militarization.

Adopting civilian-based defense may reduce the dangers of nuclear war in two ways. First, countries that possess or provide bases for nuclear weapons induce fear, targeting, and potentially even preemptive nuclear attacks against themselves. In contrast, countries that have fully transarmed to this policy are far less likely to be threatened or attacked with weapons of mass destruction, as discussed in Chapter 4.

Second, civilian-based defense potentially provides in specific cases a substitute for nuclear weapons to achieve self-reliance in deterrence and defense where conventional military means are perceived to be inadequate or impractical. Thereby the new policy could reduce pressures for nuclear proliferation. The development of nuclear weapons by France and China, and the interest in them by Israel, Taiwan, and South Korea, appear to have been closely related to dissatisfaction with dependence for security on others and to be an attempt to gain self-reliance by going the nuclear route. If this civilian-based alternative can be combined with an image of being not only effective but also more "gutsy" and a key to enhanced international status, it may provide a way to slow down and perhaps even reverse the proliferation of nuclear weapons among states.

NATO members which simply added a civilian-based defense component while retaining both their conventional military forces and nuclear weapons or bases would not reduce the nuclear dangers threatening them nor gain greater self-reliance. However, if individual European NATO members added a significant civilian-based defense component while they retained their conventional military weaponry, but also explicitly barred all nuclear possession, basing, and storage on their territory, that shift would (if believed) be likely to reduce the nuclear dangers facing them.

The United States might then, at their request, desist from threats of first-strike nuclear attacks on the Soviet Union in case of conventional attacks on those countries, or it might continue the so-called "nuclear guarantees." Should NATO not be sufficiently flexible to encourage or permit countries to add significant civilian-based defense components and to opt out of the nuclear parts of the alliance strategy, some countries might withdraw from NATO completely, relying in part or in full on the new policy for greater self-reliance in security, by means unlikely to arouse nuclear wrath.

Civilian-based defense is designed and likely to create a very high degree of self-reliance in defense and dissuasion (including deterrence) in all countries which adopt it, including small and medium-sized ones. The policy does this by shifting the decisive factor in defense from military to societal strength, thereby eliminating possession of massive and highly expensive military hardware as the requirement for self-reliance in security. Self-reliance by nonmilitary defense combines a significant reduction in the danger of annihilation in a war waged primarily by others for their own objectives, with restoration of control over defense decisions and capacities to the people of the society itself. This is true for small as well as larger countries.

If the nations of Western Europe transarmed and were consequently able to defend their societies predominantly by their own efforts—and above all without military assistance from the nuclear powers—the security problems of Europe would be altered fundamentally. This self-reliance, combined with reduced danger of annihilation, would have great advantages both to the countries with the policy and to their neighbors. The new posture would simultaneously increase their security and reduce chances of an expanding war and nuclear escalation.

We have seen that with civilian-based defense, even when deterrence fails and a defense struggle is required to repel aggression, the conflict is likely to have less harmful long-term consequences on the international system than a war. This is in part because the civilian-based defense struggle continues to focus attention on the original objective of defense, not on destruction and killing. Also, the fewer casualties and less destruction in civilian-based defense, as compared to wars, mean that there is comparatively less basis for creating lasting hatreds. Reduced long-term enmity is also more likely because of the emphasis in civilian-based defense on seeing the attackers not simply as an evil political system intent upon harm, but also as including individuals who may be vulnerable to influences from the defenders to shift their loyalties, to become less brutal in repression, and even to mutiny. Efforts by the defenders to present themselves to the leadership and general population of the attacking state as inappropriate targets for attack and repression are also likely to reduce long-term animosities.

By its nonmilitary nature, the civilian-based defense policy reduces international and internal anxieties and dangers because it provides the deterrence and defense capabilities of military systems without their capabilities to attack and repress. Unlike most military preparations, civilian-based defense cannot be used for international military aggression, or be misperceived as so intended.[12] This difference is very important in changing the international climate of fear and aggressive responses. In many past situations, military preparations intended to be defensive have been seen as aggressive. That has tended to stimulate preparations to counter them—ones also intended to defend but which again were perceived to be for attack. The result has often been an escalation of fears and military preparations, resulting in war which neither side wanted.

Civilian-based defense breaks that escalating spiral. A constant component of the tensions between the North Atlantic Treaty Organization and the Warsaw Treaty Organization is precisely that each claims that its military preparations are defensive, required by the offensive intent and preparations of the other side. It is exceptionally difficult or impossible to break that set of perceptions as long as the deterrence and defense preparations of each side can also be used to attack the other. Adoption of a strictly defensive posture by either side through civilian-based defense would drastically alter that situation. The new policy would make significant contributions to reduced international dangers in Europe and to achievement of world peace. This generally applies whether the Soviet military policies have in fact been primarily aggressively motivated (as some believe) or defensively motivated (as others believe).

In that context, let us look at the possible consequences of a Western European adoption of civilian-based defense, with the assumption that the Soviet Union's military preparations and actions have been largely stimulated by foreign military dangers—a more sympathetic view than that generally assumed in this book. From this perspective, the dangers the Soviet Union has faced may be seen by Soviet leaders as coming from NATO as a whole, the United States specifically, or a future revanchist militarized Germany. The perceived Soviet desire to avoid war is seen as rooted in memories of the terrible casualties and destruction during the Second World War.

If that has been the major motivation behind Soviet and WTO military preparations and actions, NATO countries have nevertheless perceived them to a significant degree as offensively motivated, and the Soviet Union as a potential aggressor. Given that situation, supposedly rooted in misperceptions, the transarmament of NATO as a whole or major alliance members, along with some nonaligned countries, would lead to beneficial consequences greater than simply the absence of an attack on Western Europe. Western European adoption of a security policy with a deterrence and defensive capacity against coups and invasions, a dissuasive capacity against nuclear attacks, but without a military attack capacity to threaten Eastern Europe and the Soviet Union, should significantly assuage any Soviet fears of an attack from Western Europe. A Soviet military policy change toward a less hostile orientation would then logically follow, with reduced military preparations directed toward the West.

If the Soviet political system's dictatorial characteristics have developed to a significant degree, as Stalin claimed, from fear of Western military attack, then internal relaxation could also follow. Only if there were other reasons for the repressive nature of its internal political system would the Soviet Union need to fear the general spread of knowledge of nonviolent struggle, as discussed at the beginning of this chapter. If not, a shift to a less hostile military policy and a less repressive internal political system would logically follow.

A less hostile military policy and a less repressive political system should then contribute to improved relations between the Soviet Union and Western European countries and the United States. Reduced military preparations directed toward Western Europe should—depending on the current situation with China, South Asia, and the United States—permit a reduction of Soviet military expenditures. That, in turn, should strengthen the Soviet economy, which has had serious problems, and permit improved economic conditions for the Soviet population.

Without a perceived military threat from Western Europe, the Soviet Union might be more able to relax its hold on Eastern Europe, permitting greater autonomy and democratization. Another consequence of Western European transarmament and these reactions by the Soviet Union might be improved diplomatic relationships between the Soviet Union and both Western European countries and the United States, without those relationships involving subordination to Soviet policies. This would produce a more substantive and durable détente. This situation would greatly facilitate arms control and reduction negotiations between the United States, the Soviet Union, and perhaps others. All these movements toward improved relationships and reduced tensions would be facilitated by the civilian-based defense countries' adopting a defensive political stance, instead of an offensive one, as discussed in Chapter 3.

Suppose, however, that the major assumption underlying that whole projection is not true, and that the Soviet Union's military preparations and actions have been and remain primarily aggressively oriented—as Western policy makers and others generally assume. Civilian-based defense would still be able to make positive contributions to European and wider international relations, while providing deterrence and defense capability. In this case, the improved relationships might require greater time to develop.

The worst contingency in the short run would be a pre-emptive invasion of a country which is in the midst of transarming. (Possible pre-emptive invasions in the context of an offensive political stance by the civilian-based defense country are discussed in Chapter 3.) The likely aim of such an invasion would be to prevent full preparations for civilian-based defense in that country and also to halt the spread of knowledge of nonviolent struggle from the West into the Soviet Union and Eastern Europe.

Such an invasion would probably fail, however. It is probable that at an early stage of transarmament, the military capacity would still be in place, and could be used against the Soviet attack, even though the Soviet forces and weaponry would be stronger. However, the likelihood of using that military option might be less if the transarming society had already decided to move fully to the new policy. That country might choose to apply instead the inadequately prepared nonviolent struggle capacity. In this case, by the time a society had seriously considered civilian-based defense and started the phased process of transarmament, the nature of nonviolent struggle would already be sufficiently understood to create favorable conditions for improvised nonviolent defense struggle. Then the dynamics of civilian-based defense would come into operation, as already discussed. At worst, that situation would still be preferable to nuclear war in Europe, which is a very possible consequence of NATO's present plans for repelling Soviet aggression. Using largely improvised noncooperation and defiance, the attacked society would have a good base for repelling the aggression and regaining its autonomy.

Such a pre-emptive invasion, however, is highly improbable. This is strongly suggested by the absence of a Soviet invasion of Poland during 1980, 1981 and 1982. Despite the threat posed by the nonviolent Solidarity movement to the Polish Communist system and despite Poland's being already within the Soviet military and political orbit, there was no invasion.

While a Soviet pre-emptive invasion might not be launched during Western European civilian-based defense preparations, the danger of attack might not be over. If transarmament proceeds to completion, and nevertheless the Soviet military capacity is continued at its previous level or even expanded, then clearly the transarmed Western European countries would need to develop the strongest civilian-based deterrence and defense capacities possible.

Despite the reasons already presented as to why the Soviet Union—as well as other potential attackers—would likely be deterred, it is possible that it might not be, especially in the early years of trans-armament of Western European countries. It might be necessary for the potential Soviet—or other—aggressors to learn by experience that this new policy was strong. Soviet leaders might need to be taught a lesson that neither support for coups d'état in Western European countries nor military invasions and occupations of them would achieve Soviet goals. To the contrary, such aggression would instead be harmful to the Soviet Union, not only in terms of achieving the goals of the Soviet leaders, but also for the stability and longevity of their own regime. By such lessons Soviet officials would soon learn that aggression does not pay.

Once the lesson that aggression does not pay is well learned, it is likely to reduce significantly the number of instances of international aggression, not only by the Soviet Union but also by others. Future would-be conquerors are unlikely to invade civilian-based defense countries able to defeat their aggression, deny them their objectives, sow disaffection among the attacking personnel, and prove to be politically indigestible. Aggression likely to fail is not worth the effort. Hence, one long-term international effect of civilian-based defense in Western Europe will be to lessen significantly the incidence of foreign invasions and occupations. That achievement is likely to contribute to improved international relations and goodwill, making it possible to cooperate on common interests and to resolve problems and conflicts without war and aggression.

Civilian-based defense, by providing effective deterrence and defense through nonviolent means, enables countries in this dangerous world to abandon military capacity as no longer needed. As more and more societies add civilian-based defense components to their overall security policies, gradually upgrade them, and finally abandon military capacity as counterproductive for national security, these developments will make possible a step-by-step abandonment of war.

NEXT STEPS

In conclusion, let us review some of the factors which make transarmament to civilian-based defense possible, and some of the initial steps which can be taken in that direction.

The motives for adopting and implementing civilian-based defense would include the same ones that apply in military defense. These are love of one's country, belief in the right of people to choose their own political system and government, and opposition to international aggression, internal usurpations, and foreign domination.

A society which has long relied on military means might transarm to civilian-based defense because it recognizes the limitations of military means of defense against possible attackers and expects greater chances of success by use of this very different weapons system to repel aggression. The society might want increased self-reliance in defense and foreign policies, lower destruction and loss of life in case of aggression, or major economic advantages.

An important factor in a decision to transarm must necessarily be that civilian-based defense will both directly and indirectly enhance the future security of the country. Recognition of the practical advantages of the new policy is of prime importance. Once the civilian-based defense policy is accepted as having practical advantages in preventing and defending against attacks, its nonviolent nature is likely to inspire endorsements of it as ethically or morally superior to options which depend on inflicting destruction and death. As discussed in Chapter 2, however, endorsements of the new policy as ethically superior prior to the recognition of its practical advantages are unlikely to lead to its acceptance.

The effects of the policy on the nature of the society itself may also be seen to be more beneficial than those of the military options. In addition, the society may accept the view that civilian-based defense provides a way out of the spiralling development of military technology and the nuclear arms race, and a way to move toward reducing and discarding weapons of mass destruction.

Consideration and adoption of civilian-based defense is facilitated by the fact that it does not require people to accept a new political doctrine, party program, or religion—much less to believe in nonviolence as a religious principle. Civilian-based defense does require, of course, that people be genuinely concerned with the defense and security of their society, rather than with other goals for which military means have been used, such as providing an attack capacity.

In summary, if we examine the power potential of nonviolent struggle against coups and foreign occupations, the inadequacies of present policies, and the great military capacities available to the Soviet Union, we find that strong reasons exist for Western European countries to begin, as a minimum step, to add civilian-based components to existing defense and deterrence policies. In countries where such components already exist to a limited degree—as in Switzerland, Sweden, and Yugoslavia—they need to be made more explicit and to be more adequately prepared.[13] Decisions can be made later on whether and how much to expand those components, and still later on whether to transarm fully. Obviously, there are a multitude of difficult problems involved in civilian-based defense. All these need careful examination and evaluation to determine whether they can be solved, and, if so, how.[14]

The policy, and the prospect that it may be a viable supplemental or primary policy for some Western European countries, should not frighten supporters of present defense policies for Western European countries. If civilian-based defense is indeed weak, ineffective, or counterproductive, more intensive and detailed explorations of the policy will reveal those inadequacies. The policy would in that case doubtless be rejected in favor of present policies or other options.

If, on the other hand, civilian-based defense proves viable and the Western European nations are capable of deterring attack and defending themselves with this policy, then all countries which respect international security and freedom should be pleased. The United States would be relieved of a very costly obligation. Meanwhile, the abilities of the European peoples to deter and defeat Communist and other aggression directly on the political level would be increased, making them able to defeat the objectives of any attack and inflict serious political and other costs in the process.

Nonaligned countries and individual European members of NATO should initiate or intensify their own research, policy studies, and evaluation of the potential of this policy to meet their security needs. In the United States, the government and private bodies could greatly assist this effort by launching research and policy studies on the policy and its potential for solving Western European security problems. The U.S. could encourage its European allies to do likewise, if they have not already done so. The Americans and Europeans could examine the potential international consequences of partial and full transarmament in Europe and prepare recommendations for U.S. policy during and in response to those changes.

Concerned individuals and institutions in each country can launch— parallel to these efforts or even earlier—large-scale programs of self-education and public education about the nature of the policy, the claims that have been made for it, and the ways in which the policy might best be evaluated.[15]

Can civilian-based defense meet the defense and security needs of Western European countries more adequately and with fewer grave problems than present policies? The research and policy studies recommended here are required to help answer that question definitively. But, even at this stage, grounds exist for placing hope in this new policy. Europeans of various nations have had experience with improvised nonviolent struggles against oppression, tyranny, and aggression, including under Nazi and Communist rule. We can learn from those experiences in preparing the new policy.

Civilian-based defense taps a crucial insight into the nature of power: all political power is rooted in and continually dependent upon the cooperation and obedience of the subjects and institutions of the society. That cooperation and obedience can be withdrawn. It is an insight which may have political consequences wider and deeper than the idea—which nuclear physicists were pondering in 1939—that the power locked in atoms could be released.

We have important indications that it is indeed possible for whole societies to apply that insight about political power against internal and foreign aggressors, and to triumph. Those societies can thereby contribute to the prevention and disintegration of dictatorships, enrich and expand political freedom, and help to preserve human life and achieve world peace. With effort, risks, and costs, it is possible for Europeans—and all peoples—to make themselves politically indigestible to would-be tyrants. That process has already begun. We can continue it and, building on sound foundations, succeed in making Europe unconquerable.

NOTES

NOTES TO CHAPTER 1

1. Both the extent of governmental consideration of nonviolent resistance for national defense and the degree to which it is already accepted as a component in existing policies are much greater than is generally known. A series of monographs and translations of existing government documents from European countries is in preparation. Persons wishing to receive notification of the details of their availability should write to: European Monographs, Program on Nonviolent Sanctions, Center for International Affairs, Harvard University, 1737 Cambridge Street, Cambridge, Massachusetts 02138, USA.

2. Letter dated 30 July 1982 from William P. Clark to Clare Booth Luce, concerning the first draft of the pastoral letter then in preparation by the Committee on Peace and War of the National Conference of Catholic Bishops. The letter was reported in part in Richard Halloran, "Bishops Joining Nuclear Arms Debate," 'New York Times,' 4 October 1982.

3. See D.J. Goodspeed, "The Coup d'Etat," in Adam Roberts, editor, 'The Strategy of Civilian Defence' (London: Faber & Faber, 1967); American edition: 'Civilian Resistance as a National Defense' (Harrisburg, Pa.: Stackpole Books, 1968), pp. 31–46; and Adam Roberts, "Civil Resistance to Military Coups" in 'Journal of Peace Research' (Oslo), vol. XII, no. 1, 1975, pp. 19–36. On the structural condition which makes coups possible, see Gene Sharp, "The Societal Imperative," in 'Social Power and Political Freedom' (Boston: Porter Sargent, 1980), pp. 285–308.

4. General Bernard Rogers, "For the Common Defense," in 'Harvard International Review,' vol. IV, no. 7 (May-June 1982), p. 8.

5. Bernard Brodie, 'Strategy in the Missile Age' (Santa Monica, Calif.: The Rand Corporation, R-335, 15 January 1959), p. 292.

6. Glen Snyder, 'Deterrence and Defense' (Princeton, N.J.: Princeton University Press, 1961), p. 63.

7. These statements are based on the research of William B. Vogele, who used Department of Defense data; Senate Armed Services Committee, 'Department of Defense Authorizations for Appropriations for Fiscal Year 1982,' pp. 61-68 and 101; and Arms Control and Disarmament Agency, 'World Military Expenditures and Arms Transfers 1969-1978 (1980).'

8. The Boston Study Group, 'The Price of Defense: A New Strategy for Military Spending' (New York: Times Books, 1979), p. 157.

9. Richard Halloran, "Europe Called Main U.S. Arms Cost," the 'New York Times,' 20 July, 1984, p. 2.

10. Office of Management and Budget, "O.M.B. Midsession Review of the 1985 Budget" (released 15 August, 1984), and a Congressional Budget Office release of 6 August, 1984. Both of these are courtesy of James Berchtold of the office of Senator Mark Hatfield.

11. Leonard Silk, "Reagan Budget Tightens Lid on Social Spending," the 'New York Times,' 3 February, 1985, Section 4, p. 1.

12. John J. Mearsheimer, "Why the Soviets Can't Win Quickly in Central Europe," in 'International Security,' vol. 7, no. 1 (Summer 1982), pp. 36 and 3. See n. 3 for references to arguments that NATO now has the ability to defend itself against Soviet conventional attack.

13. Ibid., pp. 3-4. See n. 4 for discussion of reasons why the Soviet Union would want to avoid a war of attrition.

14. See, for example, Michael Klare, "The Conventional Buildup" in 'Inquiry' (San Francisco), June 1983, pp. 15-17.

15. See, for example, "Do you sincerely want to be non-nuclear?" in 'The Economist' (London), 31 July 1982, pp. 30-32.

16. McGeorge Bundy, George F. Kennan, Robert S. McNamara, and Gerard Smith, "Nuclear Weapons and the Atlantic Alliance," 'Foreign Affairs,' vol. 60, no. 4 (Spring 1982), pp. 753-768.

17. Secretary Alexander Haig, "Peace and Deterrence," an address before Georgetown University's Center for Strategic and International Studies, 6 April 1982. Washington, D.C.: United States Department of State, Bureau of Public Affairs, Current Policy No. 383, p. 2.

18. European Security Study, 'Strengthening Conventional Deterrence in Europe: Proposals for the 1980s' (New York: St. Martin's Press, 1983), p. 8.

19. Ibid., p. 19.

20. Ibid., p. 8.

21. Ibid., p. 9.
22. 'Department of Defense Dictionary of Military and Associated Terms,' issued by the Joint Chiefs of Staff. J.C.S. Pub. 1., new edition 1 April 1984. Washington, D.C.: U.S. Government Printing Office. This dictionary does, however, contain entries for both 'security' and 'national security.' Portions of those definitions come close to meanings of 'defense,' but are not really the same.
23. This definition is compatible with those of Clausewitz, Liddell Hart, and Snyder. See Karl von Clausewitz, 'On War.' Trans. by Col. J.J. Graham (London: Kegan Paul, Trench, Trubner, & Co., and New York: E.P. Dutton, 1918) vol. II, pp. 133–134; B.H. Liddell Hart, 'Defense of the West' (New York: William Morrow, 1950), p. 85; and Snyder, 'Deterrence and Defense,' pp. 3–4.

"The need to *choose* between deterrence and defense is largely the result of the development of nuclear and thermonuclear weapons and long-range airpower. Prior to these developments, the three primary functions of military force—to *punish* the enemy, to *deny* him territory (or to take it back from him), and to *mitigate damage* to oneself—were embodied, more or less, in the same weapons. Deterrence was accomplished (to the extent that military capabilities were the instruments of deterrence) either by convincing the prospective aggressor that his territorial aim was likely to be frustrated, or by posing for him a prospect of intolerable costs, or both, but both of these deterrent functions were performed by the *same* forces. Moreover, these same forces were also the instruments of defense if deterrence failed." Snyder, 'Deterrence and Defense,' p. 8 Emphases in the original.
24. Nuclear weapons, Snyder pointed out, have both separated "the functions of punishment and denial" and enormously magnified the capacity for punishment. Snyder, 'Deterrence and Defense,' p. 42.
25. The three basic defensive postures applied singly or in combinations produce seven available main options: (1) conventional military defense; (2) conventional military defense combined with guerrilla defense; (3) guerrilla defense; (4) conventional military defense combined with guerrilla defense and civilian-based defense; (5) conventional military defense combined with civilian-based defense; (6) guerrilla defense combined with civilian-based defense; and (7) civilian-based defense.

For a discussion of option four, see Dietrich Fischer, "Invulnerability Without Threat: The Swiss Concept of General Defense," 'Journal of Peace Research' (Oslo), vol. XIX, no. 3 (1982), pp. 205–225. That article has been reprinted in Burns H. Weston, editor, 'Toward Nuclear Disarmament and Global Security: A Search for Alternatives' (Boulder, Colorado: Westview Press, 1984), pp. 504–532. Others seeking alternatives to present policies have limited their consideration to military options; see, for example, Bert V.A. Röling, "Feasibility of Inoffensive Deterrence," 'Bulletin of Peace Proposals' (Oslo), vol. IX, no. 4 (1978), pp. 339–347, and Frank Barnaby and Egbert Boeker, 'Defence Without Offence: Nonnuclear Defence for Europe.' Bradford University Peace Studies Series. London: Housmans Bookshop, 1982.

For discussion of option five, see Anders Boserup and Andrew Mack, 'War Without Weapons: Non-violence in National Defense' (London: Francis Pinter, 1974 and New York: Schocken, 1975), pp. 140-147; and Adam Roberts, 'Total Defence and Civil Resistance: Problems of Sweden's Security Policy' (duplicated) (Stockholm: Försvaretsforskningsanstalt, FOA P Rapport, C8335/M, September 1972), pp. 171–179, and (in Swedish) 'Totalförsvar och civil motstånd' (Stockholm: Centralforbundet Folk och Försvar, 1972), pp. 227–236.

NOTES TO CHAPTER 2

1. The account of resistance to the Kapp 'Putsch' is based on Wilfred Harris Crook, 'The General Strike' (Chapel Hill: University of North Carolina Press, 1931), pp. 496–527; Donald Goodspeed, 'The Conspirators' (New York: Viking, 1962), pp. 108–188; Erich Eyck, 'A History of the Weimar Republic' (Cambridge, Mass.: Harvard University Press, 1962), Vol. I, pp. 129–160; Karl Roloff (pseud.: Karl Ehrlich), "Den Ikkevoldelige Modstand: den Kvalte Kapp-Kupet," in Karl Ehrlich, Niels Lindberg, and Gammelgaard Jacobsen, 'Kamp Uden Vaaben: Ikke-Vold som Kampmiddel mod Krig og Undertrykkelse' (Copenhagen: Leven & Munksgaard, Einar Munksgaard, 1937), pp. 194-213; and John Wheeler-Bennett, 'The Nemesis of Power' (New York: St. Martin's Press, 1953), pp. 63–82. See also Gene Sharp, 'The Politics of Nonviolent Action' (Boston: Porter Sargent, 1973), pp. 40–41 and 79–81.

2. The account of resistance to the coup d'état in French Algeria is based upon that of Adam Roberts, "Civil Resistance to Military Coups," 'Journal of Peace Research' (Oslo), 1975, no. 1, pp. 23–30. All quotations are from that source.

3. The description of the Ruhr struggle is based on that of Wolfgang Sternstein, "The 'Ruhrkampf' of 1923" in Adam Roberts, editor, 'The Strategy of Civilian Defence' (London: Faber & Faber, 1967); American edition: 'Civilian Resistance as a National Defense' (Harrisburg, Pa.: Stackpole Books, 1968), pp. 106–135.

4. The account of Czechoslovak resistance is based on Robert Littell, editor, 'The Czech Black Book' (New York: Praeger, 1969); Robin Remington, editor, 'Winter in Prague' (Cambridge, Mass: M.I.T. Press, 1969); and Philip Windsor and Adam Roberts, 'Czechoslovakia 1968' (New York: Columbia University Press, 1969). See also Vladimir Horsky, 'Prag 1968:

Systemveränderung und Systemverteidigung' (Stuttgart: Ernst Klett Verlag and Munich: Kösel-Verlag, 1975).

5. Auguste Comte, 'The Positive Philosophy of August Comte' (Freely translated and condensed by Harriet Martineau, with an Introduction by Frederic Harrison. London: George Bell & Sons, 1896), vol. II, pp. 222–223.

6. Charles Louis de Secondat, Baron de Montesquieu, 'The Spirit of the Laws' (Translated by Thomas Nugent. Introduction by Franz Neumann. New York: Hafner, 1949), vol. I, p. 313.

7. For a fuller presentation of this theory of power, see Gene Sharp, "The Nature and Control of Political Power," in 'The Politics of Nonviolent Action," pp. 7–62, and "Social Power and Political Freedom," in 'Social Power and Political Freedom' (Boston: Porter Sargent, 1980), pp. 21–67.

8. See Gene Sharp, "Nonviolent Action: An Active Technique of Struggle," in 'The Politics of Nonviolent Action,' pp. 63–105; and ibid., passim.

9. Most of these examples from before 1972 are described, briefly or at length, with cited introductory sources, in Gene Sharp, 'The Politics of Nonviolent Action.'

10. On the nature, theory of power, methods, and dynamics of nonviolent action, see Gene Sharp, 'The Politics of Nonviolent Action.'

The technique of nonviolent action on which civilian-based defense is based may be relatively unfamiliar to many readers. That technique has been historically neglected and politically misunderstood. The brief explanatory passages about its dynamics and relevant historical cases possible in this chapter are necessarily inadequate to correct past neglect. Therefore, the reader has been referred to various sections of the author's 'The Politics of Nonviolent Action' (924 pp.). Extensive historical evidence of the power potential of nonviolent struggle can be found therein, along with detailed analyses supporting certain assertions in this volume.

No comprehensive history of nonviolent struggle has been written. Various cases are described in the following sources: Karl Ehrlich, Niels Lindberg and Gammelgaard Jacobsen, 'Kamp Uden Vaaben'; Barthélemy de Ligt, 'The Conquest of Violence: An Essay on War and Revolution' (New York: E.P. Dutton, 1938, London: Routledge, 1937, and New York and London: Garland Publishing, 1972); Clarence Marsh Case, 'Non-Violent Coercion: A Study of Methods of Social Pressure," pp. 285–396 (New York: Century Co., 1923, London: Allen & Unwin, 1923, and New York and London: Garland Publishing, 1972); Adam Roberts, editor, 'Civilian Resistance as a National Defense'; Gene Sharp, 'The Politics of Nonviolent Action'; and Gene Sharp, " 'The Political Equivalent of War'—Civilian-based Defense," in 'Social Power and Political Freedom,' pp. 195–261.

For bibliographies of accounts of cases of nonviolent struggle, see the brief one in Gene Sharp, "For Further Reading," in 'Exploring Nonviolent Alternatives' (Boston: Porter Sargent, 1970), pp. 133–159. An extensive annotated, classified bibliography of relevant books in English is in preparation. For notification when it is available, send a postcard to Bibliography, Program on Nonviolent Sanctions, Center for International Affairs, Harvard University, 1737 Cambridge Street, Cambridge, Massachusetts 02138, USA.

11. See the various publications on the topic listed in the Bibliography of this book, from Australia, Austria, Britain, Denmark, Finland, Germany, India, Japan, the Netherlands, Norway, Sweden, and the United States of America. The literature about the policy varies, with differing primary emphases, such as problems of defense, social change, war and peace, and normative considerations.

12. On belief systems that reject violence, see Gene Sharp, "Types of Principled Nonviolence," in 'Gandhi as a Political Strategist, with Essays on Ethics and Politics' (Boston: Porter Sargent Publishers, 1979), pp. 201–234.

NOTES TO CHAPTER 3

1. For other discussions of transarmament, see Adam Roberts, "Transarmament to Civilian Defence," in Adam Roberts, editor, 'The Strategy of Civilian Defence' (U.S. edition: 'Civilian Resistance as a National Defense'), pp. 291–301, and Gene Sharp, " 'The Political Equivalent of War'—Civilian-based Defense," in "Social Power and Political Freedom,' pp. 250–254.

2. On secrecy and openness in nonviolent struggle, see Gene Sharp, 'The Politics of Nonviolent Action,' pp. 481–492.

3. For introductory discussions on preparations and training, see Theodor Ebert, "Organization in Civilian Defence" in Adam Roberts, editor, 'The Strategy of Civilian Defence' (U.S. edition: 'Civilian Resistance as a National Defense'), pp. 255–273, and Gene Sharp, " 'The Political Equivalent of War'—Civilian-based Defense," in 'Social Power and Political Freedom,' pp. 237–240.

4. On the Swiss preparations for supply of food and fuel in such situations see Dietrich Fischer, "Invulnerability Without Threat: The Swiss Concept of General Defense," 'Journal of Peace Research' (Oslo), vol. XIX, no. 3 (1982). That article has been reprinted in Burns H. Weston, editor, 'Toward Nuclear Disarmament and Global Security: A Search for Alternatives' (Boulder, Colorado: Westview Press, 1984), pp. 504–532. See also 'General Defense: Interim report of the Federal Council to the Federal Assembly on the security policy of Switzerland (of December 3, 1979) (Bern: Zentralstelle für Gesamtverteidigung, December 1979), pp. 29–33.

5. For examination (outside the context of transarmament) of the problems and prospects of economic conversion from a military-oriented economy to a civilian economy, see Lloyd J. Dumas, editor, 'The Political Economy

of Arms Reduction: Reversing Economic Decay.' American Association for the Advancement of Science Selected Symposium No. 80. (Boulder, Colorado: Westview Press, 1982), and Seymour Melman, 'The Permanent War Economy' (New York: Simon and Schuster, 1974).

6. Commander Sir Stephen King-Hall, 'Defence in the Nuclear Age' (London: Victor Gollancz, 1958, and Nyack, N.Y.: Fellowship, 1959), p. 145.

7. See Gene Sharp, "The Redistribution of Power," in 'The Politics of Nonviolent Action,' pp. 777–806.

8. For a discussion of the relationships between political conditions and this policy, see April Carter, "Political Conditions for Civilian Defence," in Adam Roberts, editor, 'The Strategy of Civilian Defence' ('Civilian Resistance as a National Defense'), pp. 274–290. For a discussion on the relationship between nonviolent struggle generally and social and political structure, see Gene Sharp, 'The Politics of Nonviolent Action,' pp. 799–806, and Gene Sharp, 'Social Power and Political Freedom," pp. 342–356.

9. As quoted in Isaac Deutscher, 'Stalin: A Political Biography' (London: Oxford University Press, 1949), p. 263. See also pp. 258, 226, and 285. For further discussion and citation of Lenin on ultimate defeat of conquerors by the conquered, see Gene Sharp, 'Social Power and Political Freedom,' pp. 252–253.

NOTES TO CHAPTER 4

1. See D.J. Goodspeed, "The Coup d'Etat," in Adam Roberts, editor, 'The Strategy of Civilian Defence' (U.S. edition: 'Civilian Resistance as a National Defense'), pp. 31–46, and Adam Roberts, "Civil Resistance to Military Coups" in 'Journal of Peace Research' (Oslo), vol. XII, no. 1, 1975, pp. 19–36.

2. See Roberts, "Civil Resistance to Military Coups."

3. George F. Kennan, 'Russia and the West Under Lenin and Stalin' (London: Hutchinson, 1961 and Boston: Little, Brown & Co., 1961), p. 276.

4. See Gene Sharp, "Political 'Jiu-jitsu' " in 'The Politics of Nonviolent Action,' pp. 657–703. 'Jiu-jitsu' is a type of unarmed physical combat developed in ancient Japan which uses the oponent's strength to his disadvantage by throwing him physically off balance.

5. On Soviet troop disaffection and mutiny in 1953 in East Germany, see Stefan Brant, 'The East German Rising' (London: Thames and Hudson, 1955 and New York: Frederick A. Praeger, 1957), pp. 149–152 and 155. On effects of Hungarian influences on Soviet troops in 1956, see 'The Times' (London), 14 December 1956; 'The Observer' (London), 16 December 1956; M. Fejto in 'France Observateur' (Paris), 15 November 1956; 'Report of the Special Committee on the Problem of Hungary,' General Assembly, Official Records: Eleventh Session, Supplement No. 18 (A/3592) (New York: United Nations, 1957); and William Robert Miller, "Non-

violence: A Christian Interpretation' (New York: Association Press, 1964), pp. 357–358.

6. On the rapid rotation of Soviet troops out of Czechoslovakia, see Robert Littell, editor, 'The Czech Black Book,' pp. 134 and 212.

7. See Kevin Klose, "Soviets Reportedly Deactivate Reservists Near Polish Border," 'The Washington Post,' 13 February 1981, p. A33, and Richard D. Anderson, Jr., "Soviet Decision-Making and Poland," 'Problems of Communism,' vol. XXXI, no. 2 (March–April 1982), pp. 22–36. Anderson was formerly an analyst of Soviet military policy for the Central Intelligence Agency and at that writing was staff specialist for defense to Congressman Les Aspin.

8. Anderson, op. cit., p. 24.

9. Klose, op. cit.

10. Ibid.

11. Anderson, op. cit., p. 34.

12. Ibid., p. 32.

13. Ibid., p. 35.

14. For another discussion of nuclear weapons and civilian-based defense, see Anders Boserup and Andrew Mack, 'War Without Weapons,' pp. 177–182.

15. The 1964 ouster of Khrushchev from the Soviet leadership has frequently been attributed in part to his colleagues' judgment that his 1962 moves to deploy nuclear missiles in Cuba were imprudent. Actual nuclear attacks on another country might produce stronger, swifter consequences within a ruling group in a crisis.

On weaknesses and factionalism in totalitarian systems, see Ernest K. Bramsted, "Aspects of Totalitarian Systems" in Adam Roberts, editor, 'The Strategy of Civilian Defence' ('Civilian Resistance as a National Defense'), pp. 67–69, and Gene Sharp, 'Social Power and Political Freedom,' pp. 97–102.

16. For a similar view, see George F. Kennan, 'The Nuclear Delusion: Soviet-American Relations in the Atomic Age' (New York: Harper & Row, 1984), p. 71.

17. See Cresson H. Kearny, 'Nuclear War Survival Skills' (Coos Bay, Oregon: Nuclear War Survival Research Bureau, 1980).

18. On the contrasting significance of civil defense preparations in different defense contexts, see Dietrich Fischer, 'Preventing War in the Nuclear Age' (Totowa, New Jersey: Rowman & Allanheld, 1984), pp. 59–61.

NOTES TO CHAPTER 5

1. For other discussions of strategy in civilian-based defense, see Adam Roberts, "Civilian Defence Strategy," in Adam Roberts, editor, 'The Strategy of Civilian Defence' (U.S. edition: 'Civilian Resistance as a National Defense'), pp. 215–254; Theodor Ebert, "Initiating Popular Re-

sistance to Totalitarian Invasion," "The Crisis," and "Final Victory," in T. K. Mahadevan, Adam Roberts, and Gene Sharp, editors, 'Civilian Defence: An Introduction' (New Delhi: Gandhi Peace Foundation, and Bombay: Bharatiya Vidya Bhavan, 1967), pp. 158-211; and Johan Galtung, "On the Strategy of Nonmilitary Defence: Some Proposals and Problems," in 'Essays in Peace Research,' vol. II: 'Peace, War and Defence' (Copenhagen: Christian Ejlers, 1976), pp. 378-426 and 466-472.

2. Sir Basil Liddell Hart, 'The Memoirs of Captain Liddell Hart,' vol. I (London: Cassell, 1965 and New York: Putnam, 1965), esp. pp. 86-136 and 211-279; Liddell Hart, 'When Britain Goes to War: Adaptability and Mobility' (London: Faber & Faber, 1935), pp. 112-118 and 267-296; Liddell Hart, 'The Current of War' (London and Melbourne: Hutchinson & Co., 1941), pp. 92-125.

3. The term was introduced by Theodor Ebert.

4. See Robert Littell, editor, 'The Czech Black Book.' passim, and Philip Windsor and Adam Roberts, 'Czechoslovakia 1968,' pp. 111-131.

5. See Adam Roberts, "Civil Resistance to Military Coups," in 'Journal of Peace Research' (Oslo), vol. XII, no. 1, 1975, pp. 19-36.

6. See Gene Sharp, 'The Politics of Nonviolent Action,' especially the chapter "Solidarity and Discipline to Fight Repression" and its sections on "The Need for Nonviolent Behavior," "How Violence Weakens the Movement," and "Sabotage and Nonviolent Action," pp. 594-611.

7. See Gene Sharp, 'The Politics of Nonviolent Action,' especially pp. 492-510 and 815-817.

8. See Gene Sharp, "Social Power and Political Freedom," in 'Social Power and Political Freedom' (Boston: Porter Sargent Publishers, 1980), pp. 21-67.

9. See Gene Sharp, 'The Politics of Nonviolent Action,' Part Two, 'The Methods of Nonviolent Action,' pp. 107-445.

10. See Gene Sharp, "Three Ways Success May Be Achieved," in 'The Politics of Nonviolent Action," pp. 705-776.

NOTES TO CHAPTER 6

1. Gerald Reitlinger, 'The Final Solution: The Attempt to Exterminate the Jews of Europe' (New York: A.S. Barnes & Co., 1961 [1953]), p. 34.

2. See Gene Sharp, "The Lesson of Eichmann," in 'Social Power and Political Freedom,' pp. 86-89, and the sources cited.

3. Louis P. Lochner, editor and translator, 'The Goebbels Diaries 1942-1943' (Garden City, N.Y.: Doubleday & Co., 1948), p. 148.

4. See Sharp, "The Lesson of Eichmann," pp. 79-81, and the sources cited.

5. Ibid., pp. 75-79.

6. See Thomas Christian Wyller, 'Nyordning og Motstand: Organisasjones Politiske Rolle Under Okkupasjonen' (Oslo: Universitetsforlaget, 1958).

7. See Leonard Schapiro, 'The Communist Party of the Soviet Union' (London: Eyre and Spottiswoode, 1964), p. 431; Leonard Schapiro, 'The Origins of the Communist Autocracy: Political Opposition in the Soviet State: First Phase 1917–1922' (London: G. Bell and Sons, 1956), passim; Franz Neumann, 'Behemoth: The Structure and Practice of National Socialism 1933–1944' (New York: Octagon Books, 1963), passim; and Arthur Schweitzer, 'Big Business in the Third Reich' (London: Eyre and Spottiswoode, 1964), passim.

8. See, for example, Daniel Singer, 'The Road to Gdansk: Poland and the U.S.S.R.' (New York and London: Monthly Review Press, 1982), p. 192.

9. See Robert Littell, editor, 'The Czech Black Book,' pp. 19, 34, 37, 38, 63, 86–87, 88–89, 96, 104, 111, 114, 147, 152, and 168.

10. See the brief account in Chapter 2 and the sources cited.

11. See the brief account in Chapter 2 and the sources cited.

12. See Gene Sharp, 'The Politics of Nonviolent Action,' pp. 551–555.

13. See Gene Sharp, "Political 'Jiu-jitsu,'" in 'The Politics of Nonviolent Action,' pp. 657–703.

14. See Gene Sharp, "Solidarity and Discipline to Fight Repression," in 'The Politics of Nonviolent Action,' pp. 573–655. On the asymmetrical conflict situation, see also pp. 451–454 and 109–113.

15. On success and defeat in nonviolent action more generally, see Gene Sharp, 'The Politics of Nonviolent Action,' pp. 755–768.

16. Military defense is not always evaluated rigorously in terms of the degree of its success or failure to achieve the original objectives of the conflict. A tendency widely exists to set far lower standards for success by military means than by nonviolent means, or even to use very different criteria, such as military defeat of the opponent regardless of the other results, including the fate of the original issues. Nonviolent means are then evaluated by much higher standards than are ever applied to violent means, sometimes including unsubstantiated blame for any undesirable developments in later years. In other cases it is often assumed, without careful evaluation, that the nonviolent means have failed or simply prepared the way for violence.

For a related discussion of the use of violent action and nonviolent action to achieve political purposes, see Thomas C. Schelling, "Introduction" to Gene Sharp, 'The Politics of Nonviolent Action,' pp. xix–xxi.

17. See Gene Sharp, "The Redistribution of Power," in 'The Politics of Nonviolent Action,' pp. 777–814.

NOTES TO CHAPTER 7

1. This projection is compatible with the basic analysis that military means will only be abandoned if and when alternative effective means to provide

defense are available. See Gene Sharp, "Seeking a Solution to the Problem of War," in 'Social Power and Political Freedom,' pp. 263–284.

2. This has been simply a recapitulation of the incrementalist theory of how civilian-based defense might be adopted. See Chapter 3 for a fuller discussion of the change-over process, called "transarmament."

3. These three views are not accepted here for the following reasons. A conversion to principled rejection of violence is not required for a mass acceptance of nonviolent struggle for defense, and such a conversion of whole populations is extremely unlikely. A fundamental social transformation also is not a prerequisite for widespread adoption of nonviolent means of struggle for particular purposes, and such a basic social change is likely to be impossible without a prior abandonment of political violence as the society's ultimate sanction. Finally, a disaster is unnecessary before changes can be made, and such an experience could well lead to very different consequences. Instead of these views, the discussion of a change from military to civilian-based defense in this book is based on the incrementalist conception.

For more extensive discussion of these points, see Gene Sharp, 'The Politics of Nonviolent Action,' "Preface," pp. v–vi and "Nonviolent Action: An Active Technique of Struggle," pp. 63–105; Gene Sharp, "India's Lesson for the Peace Movement," in 'Gandhi as a Political Strategist, with Essays on Ethics and Politics'; the 'Postscripts' to "Gandhi's Defense Policy" and "Gandhi as a National Defense Strategist" in ibid., pp. 161–164, 191–195; and Gene Sharp, " 'The Political Equivalent of War'—Civilian-based Defense" and "Seeking a Solution to the Problem of War," in 'Social Power and Political Freedom,' pp. 195–261, 263–284; and other portions of those writings.

4. See Chapter 1, note 1.

5. Alternative Defence Commission, 'Defence Without the Bomb' (London: Taylor and Francis, 1983). See especially Chapter 7, "Strategies Against Occupation: 2. Defence by Civil Resistance," pp. 208–248.

6. In West Germany it is the Greens; in Denmark, the Socialist People's Party; in Norway, the Socialist Left Party; and in the Netherlands, the Social Democratic Party, Democrats 66, the Evangelical People's Party, the Radical Party, and the Pacifist Socialist Party.

7. See Joshua M. Epstein, "On Conventional Deterrence in Europe: Questions of Soviet Confidence," 'Orbis,' Spring 1982, pp. 71–88.

8. On the importance of the nature of a society's sanctions, see Gene Sharp, 'Social Power and Political Freedom,' especially pp. 291–306 and the section on "Sanctions and Society," pp. 325–356.

9. See the section "Diffused Power and the Nonviolent Technique," in Gene Sharp, 'The Politics of Nonviolent Action,' pp. 799–806; and Gene Sharp, 'Social Power and Political Freedom,' pp. 327 and 342ff.

10. Because of this tendency of nonviolent struggle to contribute to decentralization, some persons and groups that are convinced that high centralization is meritorious or that have strong vested interests in it may at some point oppose development of the new policy. That does not, however, mean that development and adoption of civilian-based defense is impossible. It does mean that work is required on the viability of decentralization in economics and politics, and on the practicality of civilian-based deterrence and defense. If those two capacities can be clearly established, then any continuing opposition by those with vested interests in centralization could be accurately perceived as selfishly motivated and as inconsistent with the society's overall welfare and security. Since consideration of civilian-based defense and the transarmament process are gradual processes, during those periods members of the society will progressively learn more and more about the capacity and potential of the policy. This increases the likelihood that the initial limited steps in exploration and introduction of the policy may receive widespread support, and also that at later stages some groups which earlier were unenthusiastic or opposed the policy may come around to support it.

11. See Gene Sharp, "Rethinking Politics" and "Facing Dictatorships with Confidence," in 'Social Power and Political Freedom,' pp. 1–20 and 91–112.

12. The Moroccan nonviolent invasion of the Spanish Sahara in 1975 (if it was nonviolent—reports differ) was atypical, and even when such aggressive nonviolent action occurs, it is very different from its military counterpart.

13. See Chapter 1, note 1.

14. On research areas in civilian-based defense, see Gene Sharp, "Research Areas on Nonviolent Alternatives," in 'Exploring Nonviolent Alternatives' (Boston: Porter Sargent, 1970), pp. 73–113, and Gene Sharp, "Research Areas on the Nature, Problems and Potentialities of Civilian Defence," in S.C. Biswas, editor, 'Gandhi: Theory and Practice, Social Impact and Contemporary Relevance: Proceedings of a Conference' (Simla: Indian Institute of Advanced Studies, 1969), pp. 393–413. The author in May 1983 established within the Center for International Affairs at Harvard University a new Program on Nonviolent Sanctions in Conflict and Defense where these problems and related ones can be investigated.

15. Information on educational and public outreach resources and a newsletter on civilian-based defense are available from the Association for Transarmament Studies, 3636 Lafayette Avenue, Omaha, Nebraska 68131, USA.

BIBLIOGRAPHY

Alternative Defence Commission, *Defence without the Bomb*. 311 pp. London: Taylor and Francis, 1983. New York: International Publications Service, Taylor and Francis, 1983. Especially Chapter 7, "Strategies Against Occupation: 2. Defence by Civil Resistance," pp. 208–248.

Arias, Gonzalo, et al., *¿Defensa Armada o Defensa Popular No-Violenta?* 158 pp. [Armed Defence or Popular Nonviolent Defence?] Barcelona: Hogar del Libro, 1982. First half is translation of Baudonnel et al.

Atkeson, Brigadier General Edward B., "The Relevance of Civilian-Based Defense to U.S. Security Interests," *Military Review* (Fort Leavenworth, Kansas), Vol. 56, No. 5 (May 1976), pp. 24–32, and No. 6 (June 1976), pp. 45–55.

_____, "Un Nuevo Concepto de Defensa: Su Relación de la Seguridad de E.U.," *Military Review* (Latin American edition), Vol. 56, No. 5 (May 1976), pp. 12–20, and No. 6 (June 1976), pp. 45–56 (translation of "The Relevance of Civilian-Based Defense to U.S. Security Interests").

_____, "A Defesa Baseaba no Elemento Civil," *Military Review* (Brazilian edition), Vol. 56, No. 5 (May 1976), pp. 88–97, and No. 6 (June 1976), pp. 39–50 (translation of "The Relevance of Civilian-Based Defense to U.S. Security Interests").

Baudonnel, Georges, et al., *Armée ou Défense Civile Non-violente?* [Army or Nonviolent Civilian Defence?] La Clayette: Combat Non-violent, 1975.

Bekkers, Frits and Hans W. Blom, et al., *Geweldloze Actie en Sociale Verdediging.* 159 pp. [Nonviolent Action and Social Defence]. Rotterdam: Universitaire Pers Rotterdam, 1971.

Bergfeldt, Lennart, see Swedish Commission on Nonmilitary Resistance.

Bondurant, Joan, "Paraguerrilla Strategy: A New Concept in Arms Control" in *Journal of Conflict Resolution*, 1: 235–245 (1957).

Boserup, Anders and Andrew Mack, *Ikke-vold som Nationalforsvar.* 222 pp. [Nonviolence as a National Defence]. Copenhagen: Spektrums Aktuelle, 1971.

_____, *Krieg ohne Waffen.* [War Without Weapons]. Reinbek: Rowohlt, 1974 (translation of *Ikke-vold som Nationalforsvar*).

_____, *War Without Weapons: Non-Violence in National Defence.* 194 pp. London: Francis Pinter, 1974 (translation of *Ikke-vold som Nationalforsvar*).

_____, *War Without Weapons: Non-Violence in National Defense.* 194 pp. New York: Schocken, 1975 (translation of *Ikke-vold som Nationalforsvar*).

Daim, Wilfried, *Analyse einer Illusion: Das Österreichische Bundesheer.* [Analysis of an Illusion: The Austrian Federal Army]. Bellnhausen (Federal Republic of Germany): Verlag Hinder und Deelmann, 1969.

Ebert, Theodor, ed., *Demokratische Sicherheitspolitik: Von der territorialen zur sozialen Verteidigung.* 257 pp. [Democratic Security Policy: From Territorial to Social Defence]. Munich: Carl Hanser Verlag, 1974.

_____, *Gewaltfreier Aufstand: Alternative zum Bürgerkrieg.* 408 pp. [Nonviolent Uprising: Alternative to Civil War]. Freiburg im Breisgau: Verlag Rombach, 1967; revised and abridged edition, Frankfurt am Main and Hamburg: Fischer Bücherei, 1970. 238 pp.

_____, *Soziale Verteidigung. Band 1: Historische Erfahrungen und Grundzüge der Strategie.* 193 pp. [Social Defence. Volume 1: Historical Experiences and Characteristics of the Strategy]. *Band 2: Formen und Bedingungen des zivilen Widerstandes.* 194 pp. [Volume 2: Forms and Conditions of Civil Resistance]. Waldkirch (Federal Republic of Germany): Waldkircher Verlagsgesellschaft, 1981.

_____, "Von aggressiver Drohung zu defensiver Warnung: Das Konzept der Sozialen Verteidigung," [From Aggressive Threat to Defensive Warning: The Concept of Social Defence], in Dieter Senghaas, ed., *Friedensforschung und Gesellschaftskritik.* [Peace Research and Social Criticism]. pp. 152–200. Frankfurt am Main: Fischer, 1973.

_____, ed., *Wehrpolitik ohne Waffen: Vom passiven Widerstand zur sozialen Verteidigung.* 168 pp. [Defence Policy Without Weapons: From Passive Resistance to Social Defence]. Opladen (Federal Republic of Germany): Argus Verlag, 1972.

_____, ed., *Ziviler Widerstand: Fallstudien aus der innenpolitischen Friedens — und Konfliktforschung.* 322 pp. [Civil Resistance: Case Studies from Domestic Peace and Conflict Research]. Düsseldorf: Bertelsmann Universitätsverlag, 1970.

Ebert, Theodor, J. de Graff, Gernot Jochheim, Herman de Lange, and Hylke Tromp, *Met/Zonder Alle Geweld: inleiding tot sociale verdediging.* 116 pp. [With/Instead of All Force: Introduction to Social Defence]. Utrecht-Landbroek: Schotanus Publishing Company B.V., 1972.

Feddema, J.P., A.H. Herring and E.A. Huisman, *Verdediging met een menselijk gezicht: Grondslagen en praktijk van sociale verdediging* [Defence with a

Human Face: Foundations and Practice of Social Defence]. 94 pp. Amersfoort: De Horstink. Zwolle: De Stichting Voorlichting Aktieve Geweldloosheid, 1982.

Freistetter, Franz, "Experiment gewaltfreie Verteidigung" [Nonviolent defense experiment] in Österreichische Militärische Zeitschrift [Austrian Military Journal], Vol. XI, No. 1 (January-February 1973), pp. 37-41 and No. 2 (March-April 1973), pp. 121-125.

Galtung, Johan, "On the Strategy of Nonmilitary Defense: Some Proposals and Problems," in Johan Galtung, Essays in Peace Research. Vol. II, Peace, War and Defense, pp. 378-426 and 466-472. Copenhagen: Christian Ejlers, 1976. 472 pp.

Geeraerts, Gustaaf, ed., Possibilities of Civilian Defence in Western Europe. 172 pp. Amsterdam and Lisse: Swets and Zeitlinger, 1977.

Geeraerts, Gustaaf and Patrick Stouthuysen, eds., Veiligheid en Alternative Defensie: De Idee van Sociale Verdediging [Security and Alternative Defence: The Idea of Social Defence]. 178 pp. Brussels: Internationale van Oorlogstegenstanders—Document, 1983.

Gleditsch, Nils Petter, ed., Kamp Uten Våpen. 200 pp. [Struggle Without Weapons]. Oslo: Pax Forlag, 1965.

Holst, Johan Jørgen, Eystein Fjærli and Harald Rønning, Ikke-Militært Forsvar og Norsk Sikkerhetspolitikk. [Nonmilitary Defence and Norwegian Security Policy]. Kjeller (Norway): Forsvarets Forskningsinstituut, 1967.

Höglund, Bengt, et al., Fredspolitik: Civilmotstånd. 232 pp. [The Politics of Peace: Civil Resistance]. Stockholm: Bokförlaget Aldus/Bonniers, 1969.

Kennan, George, Russia, the Atom and the West. 120 pp. London: Oxford University Press, 1958.

Keyes, Gene, "Strategic Non-Violent Defense: The Construct of an Option," The Journal of Strategic Studies (London), Vol. 4, No. 2 (June 1981), pp. 125-151.

King-Hall, Commander Sir Stephen, Common Sense in Defence. 48 pp. London: K-H Services, 1960.

_____ , Defence in the Nuclear Age. 223 pp. London: Gollancz, 1958.

_____ , Defense in the Nuclear Age. Nyack, New York: Fellowship, 1959.

_____ , Den Krieg im Frieden gewinnen. 223 pp. [To Win the War in Peace]. Hamburg: Henri Nannen, 1958 (translation of Defence in the Nuclear Age).

_____ , Power Politics in the Nuclear Age: A Policy for Britain. London: Gollancz, 1962.

Klumper, A.A., Sociale Verdediging en Nederlands Verzet '40-'45: Indeëel Concept Getoetst aan Historische Werkelijkheid [Social Defence in the Dutch Resistance '40-'45: The Ideal Concept Tested in Historical Reality]. 504 pp.

Koch, Koen, "Civilian Defence: An Alternative to Military Defence?" in The Netherlands Journal of Sociology, Vol. 20, No. 1 (April, 1984), pp. 1-12.

_____ , Sociale Verdediging: Een Kritische Literatuurbeschouwing [Social Defence: A Critical Reflection on the Literature]. 199 pp. The Hague: Begeleidingsgroep Inzake het Onderzoek op het Gebied van de Geweldloze Conflictoplossing, 1982.

Koschmann, J. Victor, "The Boundaries of Human Conflict," *The Japan Interpreter* (Tokyo), Vol. VII, Nos. 3-4 (Summer-Autumn 1972), pp. 422-431. (Review article on Mitsuo Miyata, *Hibusō kokumin teikō no shisō* [The Philosophy of Unarmed Civilian Resistance]).

Kritzer, Herbert, "Nonviolent National Defense: Concepts and Implications," *Peace Research Reviews* (Oakville, Ontario: Canadian Peace Research Institute), Vol. 5, No. 5 (April 1974), pp. 1-57.

Laine, Pentti, ed., *Siviilivastarinta.* [Civilian Resistance]. Helsinki: Tammi, 1969.

Mack, Andrew, "The Strategy of Non-Military Defence," in Desmond Ball, ed., *Strategy and Defence: Australian Essays* (Sydney: George Allen & Unwin, 1982), pp. 148-169.

_____ , see Boserup, Anders and Andrew Mack.

Mahadevan, T.K., Adam Roberts and Gene Sharp, eds., *Civilian Defence: An Introduction.* 265 pp. New Delhi: Gandhi Peace Foundation and Bombay: Bharatiya Vidya Bhavan, 1967.

Maislinger, Andreas, *Probleme der Österreichischen Verteidigungspolitik* [Problems of Austrian Defence Policy]. Unpublished dissertation. Salzburg, 1980.

Mellon, Christian, Jean-Marie Muller, Jacques Sémelin, *La Dissuasion Civile: Principes et méthodes de la résistance non violente dans la Stratégie Française.* 204 pp. Paris: Fondation pour les Études de Défense Nationale, 1985.

Miyata, Mitsuo, *Hibusō kokumin teikō no shisō.* [The Philosophy of Unarmed Civilian Resistance]. Tokyo: Iwanami shoten, 1971.

_____ , "The Japanese Constitution and Nonviolent Resistance as a National Defense," in *Peace Research in Japan*, 1972.

Muller, Jean-Marie, *Vous Avez Dit "Pacifisme"? De la menace nucléaire a la défense civile non-violente* [You Said "Pacifism"? From the Nuclear Menace to Nonviolent Civilian Defence], especially Part Two, "Vers une Défense Populaire Non-Violente" [Toward a Nonviolent Popular Defence], pp. 199-305. Paris: Les Éditions du Cerf, 1984.

Roberts, Adam, "Civil Resistance as a Technique in International Conflict" in *Yearbook of World Affairs.* London: Stevens, 1970.

_____ , "Civil Resistance to Military Coups," *Journal of Peace Research*, (Oslo), Vol. XII, No. 1 (1975), pp. 19-36.

_____ , "Civilian Defence Twenty Years On" in *Bulletin of Peace Proposals* (Oslo), Vol. 9, No. 4 (1978), pp. 293-300.

_____ , ed., *Civilian Resistance as a National Defense: Non-violent Action Against Aggression.* 320 pp. Harrisburg, Pa. (U.S.A.): Stackpole Books, 1968 (reprint of *The Strategy of Civilian Defence*).

_____ , ed., *Civilmotståndets Strategi: Historiska exempel och aktuella tillämpningar.* 335 pp. [The Strategy of Civilian Resistance: Historical Examples and Current Applications]. Stockholm: Bokförlaget Aldus/Bonniers, 1969 (abridged translation of *The Strategy of Civilian Defence*).

_____, ed., *Gewaltloser Widerstand gegen Aggressoren: Probleme, Beispiele, Strategien.* 311 pp. [Nonviolent Resistance Against Aggressors: Problems, Examples, Strategies]. Göttingen: Vandenhoeck & Ruprecht, 1971 (translation of *The Strategy of Civilian Defence*).

_____, ed., *Hele Folket i Forsvar.* 226 pp. [The Whole People in Defence]. Oslo: Pax Forlag, 1969 (abridged translation of *The Strategy of Civilian Defence*).

_____, "Jinmin teikō no susume—Nihon no anzen hoshō o saiko suru," [Promoting Popular Resistance: Rethinking Japanese Security], *Sekai* (August 1982), pp. 69–82.

_____, *Occupation, Resistance and Law: International Law on Military Occupations and on Resistance.* 311 pp. Stockholm: Försvarets Forskningsanstalt, 1980. Revised edition: Oxford and New York: Oxford University Press, 1983.

_____, *Ockuptation, Motstånd och Folkrätt.* 200 pp. [Occupation, Resistance and International Law.] Stockholm: Försvar och Säkerhetspolitik, 1981. (Swedish edition of *Occupation, Resistance and Law.*)

_____, ed., *The Strategy of Civilian Defence: Non-Violent Resistance to Aggression.* 320 pp. London: Faber & Faber, 1967. Paperback edition with new introduction: *Civilian Resistance as a National Defense: Non-violent Action Against Aggression.* 367 pp. Harmondsworth (England) and Baltimore, Md. (U.S.A.): Penguin Books, 1969.

_____, *Total Defence and Civil Resistance: Problems of Sweden's Security Policy.* FOA P Rapport C8335/M. Stockholm: Försvarets Forskningsanstalt, 1972 (English edition of *Totalförsvar och Civilmotstånd*).

_____, *Totalförsvar och Civilmotstånd.* 287 pp. Stockholm: Centralförbundet Folk och Försvar, 1972 (Swedish edition of *Total Defence and Civil Resistance*).

_____, Frank, Jerome D., Arne Naess and Gene Sharp, *Civilian Defence.* 70 pp. Foreword by the Hon. Alastair Buchan. London: Peace News, 1964.

_____, *Modstand—Uden Vold.* 100 pp. [Resistance—Without Violence]. Copenhagen: Borgen, 1965 (translation of *Civilian Defence*).

_____, (See Mahadevan, T.K., et al.).

Schmid, Alex P. *Social Defence and Soviet Military Power: An Inquiry into the Relevance of an Alternative Defence Concept.* 469 pp. Leiden (Netherlands): Center for the Study of Social Conflict, State University of Leiden, 1986, for the Ministry for the Advancement of Science.

Schwarcz, Ernest, *Mehr Sicherheit ohne Waffen II: Die Verteidigung Österreichs durch gewaltlosen Widerstand.* 94 pp. [More Security Without Weapons II: The Defence of Austria through Nonviolent Resistance]. Vienna: Sensenverlag, 1976.

Sémelin, Jacques, *Pour Sortir de la Violence* [In Order to Leave Violence]. 202 pp. Paris: Les Éditions Ouvriéres, 1983.

Sharp, Gene, *Buki naki minshū no teikō: Sono senryakuron-teki apurōch.* 268 pp. [Mass Resistance Without Weapons: Its Military-Strategic Approach]. Tokyo: Renga Shoba, 1972 (translation of *Exploring Nonviolent Alternatives*).

_____, *Exploring Nonviolent Alternatives*. 162 pp. Introduction by David Riesman. Boston: Porter Sargent, 1970.

_____, "Gandhi's Defense Policy" and "Gandhi as a National Defense Strategist," in Gene Sharp, *Gandhi as a Political Strategist, with Essays on Ethics and Politics*, pp. 131–198. Introduction by Coretta Scott King. Boston: Porter Sargent, 1979. 357 pp.

_____, "Investigating New Options in Conflict and Defense," *Teachers College Record* (Columbia University), Vol. 84, No. 1 (Fall 1982), pp. 50–64 and *Social Alternatives* (Brisbane, Australia), Vol. 3, No. 2 (March 1983), pp. 13–20. Reprinted in Douglas Sloan, ed., *Education for Peace and Disarmament: Toward a Living World*, pp. 50–64, New York and London: Teachers College Press, 1983.

_____, "Krigens Politiske Modstykke–Civilt Forsvar," in Jonassen, Hagbard, ed., *Aldrig Mere Krig* (Never Again War], pp. 89–147. Copenhagen: Borgens Forlag, 1966 (translation of " 'The Political Equivalent of War'–Civilian Defense"). 152 pp.

_____, "Making the Abolition of War a Realistic Goal" (pamphlet). 16 pp. New York: Institute for World Order, 1981.

_____, *National Security Through Civilian-Based Defense*. Omaha: Association for Transarmament Studies, 1985.

_____, *Poder, Luta, e Defesa*. [Power, Struggle, and Defence]. 272 pp. São Paulo: Edicões Paulinas, 1983.

_____, " 'The Political Equivalent of War'–Civilian Defense," *International Conciliation* (New York, Carnegie Endowment for International Peace), No. 555 (whole number), November 1965, pp. 1–67. Revised edition: " 'The Political Equivalent of War'–Civilian-based Defense," in Gene Sharp, *Social Power and Political Freedom*, pp. 195–261. Boston: Porter Sargent, 1980. 440 pp.

_____, *The Politics of Nonviolent Action*. 902 pp. Introduction by Thomas C. Schelling. Prepared under the auspices of Harvard University's Center for International Affairs. Boston: Porter Sargent, 1973. Paperback in three vols.: I, *Power and Struggle*, 105 pp.; II, *The Methods of Nonviolent Action*, 339 pp.; III, *The Dynamics of Nonviolent Action*, 457 pp. Boston: Porter Sargent, 1974.

_____, " 'Das politische Äquivalent des Krieges'–die gewaltlose Aktion," ["The Political Equivalent of War"–Nonviolent Action], in Ekkehart Krippendorff, ed., *Friedensforschung*, [Peace Research], pp. 477–513. Cologne and Berlin: Kiepenheuer & Witsch, 1968 (translation of " 'The Political Equivalent of War'–Civilian Defense"). 596 pp.

_____, *Post-Military Defense*. Princeton, New Jersey: Princeton University Press, forthcoming.

_____, "Research Areas on the Nature, Problems and Potentialities of Civilian Defence," in S.C. Biswas, ed., *Gandhi: Theory and Practice, Social Impact and Contemporary Relevance: Proceedings of a Conference*. Simla: Indian Institute of Advanced Studies, 1969, pp. 393–413.

_____ , "Research Project on 'Totalitarianism and Nonviolent Resistance,' " *Journal of Conflict Resolution* (Ann Arbor, Mich., U.S.A.), Vol. III, No. 2 (June 1959), pp. 153–161.

_____ , "Sensō no Haizetsu o Jitsugen Kanō na Mokuhyō to Surutame-ni," [Toward the Objective of Making the Abolition of War a Realizable Possibility], Translation by Tamayo Okamoto. *Gunji Minron*, [People's Military Forum], No. 28 (1 May 1982) (translation of "Making the Abolition of War a Realistic Goal").

_____ , *Sociale Verdediging: Afschrikking en Verdediging Door Burgers.* 54 pp. [Social Defence: Deterrence and Defence by Civilians]. The Hague: Stichting Maatschappij en Krijgsmacht, Winter '81/82 (translation of "Civilian-based Defense: A New Deterrence and Defense Policy," unpublished in English).

_____ , *Social Power and Political Freedom.* 440 pp. Introduction by Senator Mark O. Hatfield. Boston: Porter Sargent, 1980.

_____ , "Sociale Verdediging: Optie voor West-Europa," [Social Defence: Option for Western Europe], *JASON-magazine* (The Hague) Vol. III, No. 5 (December 1978), pp. 14–21.

_____ , (See Mahadevan, T.K. et al.).

Sveics, V.V., *Small Nation Survival: Political Defense in Unequal Conflicts.* New York: Exposition Press, 1970.

Swedish Commission on Nonmilitary Resistance, Ministry of Defence, *Kompletterande Motståndsformer.* 207 pp. [Complementary Forms of Resistance]. Includes appendices. Statens Offentliga Utredningar 1984: 10, Försvarsdepartementet. Stockholm: Liber Allmänna Förlaget, 1984. English summary: Stockholm: Försvarsdepartementet, 1984.

Thoft, Jens, ed., *Ikke-vold: Strategi i Klassekampen.* 208 pp. [Nonviolence: Strategy in the Class Struggle]. Copenhagen: Forlaget G.M.T., 1974.

Tromp, Hylke, ed., *Sociale Verdediging: Theorieen over Niet-Militaire Verdediging als Alternatief voor Geweldpolitiek en Nukleaire Afschrikking.* 256 pp. [Social Defence: Theories of Nonmilitary Defence as Alternative to Politics of Violence and Nuclear Deterrence]. Groningen, XENO, and Antwerp: Pax Christi, 1979.

Vereinigung Deutscher Wissenschaftler, *Eine andere Verteidigung? Alternativen zur Atomaren Abschreckung.* 174 pp. [Another Defence? Alternatives to Atomic Deterrence]. Munich: Carl Hanser Verlag, 1973.

_____ , *Civilian Defence: Wissenschaftliche Arbeitstagung über Civilian Defence. Voraussetzungen und Möglichkeiten. Ein neuer Weg zu Abrüstung und Sicherheit?* 192 pp. [Civilian Defence: Scientific Working Conference on Civilian Defence. Premises and Possibilities. A New Road to Disarmament and Security?] Bielefeld (Federal Republic of Germany): Bertelsmann Universitätsverlag, 1968.

Vetschera, Heinz, *Soziale Verteidigung—Ziviler Widerstand—Immerwährende Neutralität.* 268 pp. [Social Defence—Civil Resistance—Permanent Neutrality]. Vienna: Institut für Militärstrategische Grundlagenforschung, 1974.

INDEX

173

ABOUT THE AUTHOR

Gene Sharp, D.Phil. (Oxon.), directs the Program on Nonviolent Sanctions in Conflict and Defense at Harvard University's Center for International Affairs, and is President of the Albert Einstein Institution, a foundation in Cambridge, Massachusetts, devoted to research on nonviolent struggle. He was formerly Professor of Political Science and Sociology at Southeastern Massachusetts University.

Mr. Sharp holds the degree of Doctor of Philosophy in political theory from Oxford University. He lived for ten years in England and Norway before being invited to Harvard.

Mr. Sharp is the author of *The Politics of Nonviolent Action* (1973; introduction by Thomas C. Schelling), immediately hailed as the definitive study of nonviolent struggle. His other books include *Social Power and Political Freedom* (1980; introduction by Senator Mark O. Hatfield) and *Gandhi as a Political Strategist, with Essays on Ethics and Politics* (1979; introduction by Coretta Scott King).

Mr. Sharp has lectured in several Western European countries as well as in Australia, Asia, and North America. He was a consultant to the Dutch government's commission on civilian-based defense, and has lectured at several military colleges and academies. His writings have been translated into fifteen other languages.

He maintains that the major unsolved political problems of our time — dictatorship, genocide, war, social oppression, and popular powerlessness—require us to rethink politics in order to develop fresh strategies and programs for their resolution. This book is an attempt to aid the rethinking of Western European security problems.

OTHER BOOKS BY GENE SHARP

The Politics of Nonviolent Action, available also in three paperback volumes, *Power and Struggle, The Methods of Nonviolent Action*, and *The Dynamics of Nonviolent Action*. Introduction by Thomas C. Schelling.

Gandhi as a Political Strategist, with Essays on Ethics and Politics. Introduction by Coretta Scott King.

Social Power and Political Freedom. Introduction by Senator Mark O. Hatfield.

All of the above are published by Porter Sargent Publishers, 11 Beacon Street, Boston, Massachusetts 02108, USA.

National Security Through Civilian-based Defense. (96 pp.) Association for Transarmament Studies, 3636 Lafayette, Omaha, Nebraska 68131, USA.

PAMPHLET

"Making the Abolition of War a Realistic Goal." (16 pp.) The Ira D. and Miriam G. Wallach Award essay. World Policy Institute, 777 United Nations Plaza, New York, New York, 10017, USA.

For more information on Gene Sharp's books and publications in fifteen other languages, write to Publications Coordinator, Program on Nonviolent Sanctions, Center for International Affairs, Harvard University, 1737 Cambridge Street, Cambridge, Massachusetts 02138, USA.